What women
BRII

MW00681577

*"**Bring It On!** offers you tangible tools to deepen your life experience. Couched in stories, quotes, and action items, Christine's valuable wisdom promises to help you emerge as a more powerful and fulfilled person than you ever imagined."*

—Andrea H. Gold, President
Gold Stars Speakers Bureau, Tucson, AZ

*"As you travel through **Bring It On!**, you'll find yourself dealing with your emotional baggage in a way that you won't even realize you're unpacking. Christine makes the path easy to follow and offers comfort, sound advice, and food for thought along the way."*

—Judy Nauta, professional speaker

*"**Bring It On!** awakens thoughts and feelings that almost any woman in her forties and fifties can identify with and truly speaks to the heart of women at this pivotal stage of life."*

—Ellyn Davis, The Elijah Company

*"Wow! **Bring it On!** is incredibly thought provoking for women of all ages. I have already begun to incorporate the actions steps into my own life and love the continuing process of discovering who I am and learning how to live my life with more authenticity!*

—Susan Creal, Peak Performance Coaching, LLC

Bring It On!

women embracing midlife

christine carter schaap

Vineyard

ENTERPRISES, LLC

Rockford, Michigan

Bring It On!

women embracing midlife

christine carter schaap

First Printing, 2004
Printed in the United States of America
ISBN: 0-9748443-0-6
LCCN: 2004111475

Cover Design: Mike Cox
Book Design: Dawn Teagarden

Please note that many of the names in this book were changed to protect the identities of the women who so freely shared their experiences.

To Steve —
Thanks for your belief in me, your unwavering
love, and your exceptional culinary skills! Words
cannot express the depth of love and gratitude
I feel for you, honey. None of this would
have happened without you.

ACKNOWLEDGEMENTS

With heartfelt thanks and appreciation:

- ❖ To all the women who so graciously shared your stories with me — I am deeply grateful for your candidness and complete transparency.

- ❖ To my book coach, Sanyika Calloway Boyce, for your focus in shepherding this book through its final stages.

- ❖ To my editor, Pat MacEnulty, for all of your invaluable recommendations. I appreciate the skill with which you so gracefully wove the women's stories and quotes throughout this book.

- ❖ To my dear friends — Anita, Leslie, Tess, Jackie, and Patty — for your friendship, inspiration, and unparalleled support. Thanks for cheering me on!

- ❖ To our "Wendy's group" — Mark & Gertie, Dan & Kris, Jim & Machelle, Jim & Beth, and Brian & Judy — you remind me what a difference a close circle of caring friends can make. I feel honored to be part of your life!

- ❖ To Mom — for transporting your grandchildren to piano lessons, biology labs, and soccer practices so I could work on my book. I owe you so much!

- ❖ To my children — Ben, Zachary, Nicholas, Jonathan, and Alex — for the hugs, words of encouragement, and much needed shoulder massages. They were more meaningful than you know! You're awesome!

- ❖ To my Creator — for the life you've given me. It's all about you!

TABLE OF CONTENTS

INTRODUCTION:
NOTES FOR THE JOURNEY

Midlife offers a unique opportunity to reevaluate and, if necessary, correct your course — a chance to set new goals and priorities for yourself and make choices that will create the rich, satisfying experience you always hoped your life would be. It's a time to reclaim your forgotten dreams.

Whether out of a sense of duty or a desire for approval, women tend to be people pleasers. When you feel pulled in multiple, often conflicting directions, it's easy to overlook your own wants and needs. Focusing on others wears you down and leaves you feeling depleted, but thinking about what you need seems selfish — an unaffordable luxury. Navigating through a midlife transition, however, requires you to assume responsibility for your own growth and personal fulfillment.

For many women, the responsibilities of being a parent are dwindling while for others the prospect of starting a family is an ever-increasing concern. At forty, you may be a grandmother or you may have just had your first child. If your twenties and thirties were spent raising a family or developing a career — or maybe struggling to manage both — you suddenly discover that you're longing to do all the things you had to postpone for the sake of your children or work. Although those responsibilities may continue, you're now free to follow dreams you never before had time to pursue.

If you're feeling like you're in the prime of your life, you're not alone. Years ago, I remember my dad telling me that his forties and fifties were the best years of his life. He finally had enough wisdom, wealth, and experience to really enjoy living!

Dad also believed that women became more attractive at midlife as they blossomed into vibrant, self-assured individuals with passion and purpose for living. His words have stayed in the back of my mind for more than a decade and helped shape how I've approached my own middle years. Heidi, one of the women I interviewed, said, "Personally, I believe that as far as outer looks go, I look far better today than I did in my teens, even with the fine lines and gray hair!"

You probably know several women who have taken considerable risks in order to lead more authentic lives: perhaps someone who turned down a promotion to have more time with her family, forfeited a steady income to launch a new business, started a family after forty, earned a college degree in midlife, or took early retirement in order to volunteer full-time. Embracing life requires the courage to face your fears, change habits that perpetuate the life you have, and acknowledge the dreams you've kept suppressed.

In the process of researching this book, I interviewed women from all walks of life — from powerful executives to intelligent, creative stay-at-home moms. As you hear their stories, you'll likely discover several that will resonate with your own. Like you, these women possess a wealth of life experience. Though they each have found varying degrees of success, all of them recognize areas that could be improved and are gaining the courage to take risks and venture into uncharted waters.

Ann, another woman I interviewed, said she felt as if she were at a turning point. "I turned the corner and got a glimpse of myself in the mirror for the first time. With each passing day, I get a closer glimpse of who I am and I am starting to like what I see. I am grasping hold of that vision and fighting to see the real me, completely revealed."

Writing this book has been part of my personal transition into midlife. My own journey began at age thirty-seven and lasted about three years. It was marked by a period of self-reflection as I sorted out questions such as:

- What is my purpose? What gives my life meaning?
- Are my relationships as mutually satisfying as they could be?
- Does my use of time reflect my true priorities?
- How can I meet my need for creative expression?
- Is my career gratifying enough?
- Looking back in twenty years, what do I want to have accomplished with my life?
- What will I wish I'd have done more of? Less of?

Daily quiet time spent reading and journaling provided increased insights and allowed me to become more aware of my feelings and emotions. I awakened to the realization that I'd settled into a life that had become comfortable and secure — one that seemed difficult, if not impossible, to change.

Typical of many women, my early adult years were devoted to going to school, getting a job, finding a mate, raising a family, and doing my best to make everyone else happy. Eventually, however, I experienced the same pull so many women said they'd felt — the pull to examine and address my own needs.

The process wasn't always fun, but the personal growth and understanding of myself that resulted was worth every struggle, every risk, and every painful mistake on the journey to living a more authentic, faith-filled life. Midlife isn't something you can avoid, so you might as well embrace it! C'mon, bring it on!

Christine Carter Schaap
Rockford, Michigan
June 2004

CHAPTER ONE:
YOUR WAKE UP CALL

*"Don't be afraid of growing older, because as you
embrace each new season, it brings its own joys
and new opportunities for fulfillment."*
—Dianna Booher

Awareness of your discontentment

When Ginny was experiencing midlife, she was
so disappointed in her life that one day she "up and
quit!" She stopped cooking and cleaning. She
dropped everything and thought, "Why bother? No
one notices anyway."

Her husband didn't believe her when she told
him she quit, but a couple of months later he said,
"You really did quit, didn't you?"

"Yep!" she answered.

Ginny felt taken for granted. It seemed that nothing
she did for anyone was ever appreciated — or good
enough. She had reached the bottom emotionally.

"If something went wrong, I got yelled at for not taking the proper precautions to foresee it or prevent it. I felt lost — lost in an ocean of doing things for everyone else. I was overloaded and burned out," she said. "It was time to change the batteries, but the energy in these new batteries was going to be put forth in finding myself — the person I was meant to be."

Ginny spent her midlife years discovering who she was. She learned that she had to take care of herself because when she did that, and was happy with herself, everything else became much easier to deal with.

"In hindsight, quitting showed me my preoccupation with everything else. I was ignoring the changes I needed to make in my life. I was looking at external circumstances instead of looking inside of myself," she concluded.

For many women, the transition to midlife is a period of confusion and uncertainty. About the time you think your development is coming to an end, you find yourself embarking on a totally unexpected journey of growth and change.

Although a normal part of maturing, midlife represents distinctive adjustments for women:

- Losing your sense of purpose — feeling perplexed about the meaning of your life
- Shifting parental responsibilities as children are launched or need less attention
- Awareness that you're beginning to show signs of aging

- Concern about approaching menopause and how it will affect your life
- Behaving completely out-of-character — feeling like a stranger to yourself
- Bewilderment over a "crush" you've developed on someone not even your type
- Neglected talents demanding to be expressed — dreams and desires reemerging
- Boredom with activities that previously held great interest and dominated your life
- Caring for aging parents — discovering the roles are suddenly reversed
- Biological clock ticking — wondering if it's too late to start a family
- Questioning the accuracy of assumptions made years ago about God and faith

Frequently, a midlife crisis is brought on by your own internal feelings of discontentment. It's a reaction to the fear of losing your youth — your "last chance" for happiness. You wake up one morning with a profound feeling of emptiness inside, haunted by a vague sense that something is missing in your life. Suddenly you're bored with what used to interest you and dissatisfied by your relationships or in your chosen roles in life. It's not uncommon to feel depressed, lost and confused. Just knowing that this is normal can help you stay sane.

Sometimes, these emotions are a result of some significant loss or change — your husband leaves, your company downsizes, your child dies unexpectedly, or you're diagnosed with a life-threatening illness — all external events over which you have no control. After the initial shock and denial, the common reaction is to ignore it and hope it will go away. Eventually though, you will accept what has happened and consider new options, build on your strengths, and begin to regain control of your life.

For me, midlife was a time of great awakening — a time when my spirit demanded to be heard and rose from the noises of everyday life. At first there was great confusion until I put a label on my changing awareness of life . . . "MIDLIFE CRISIS." Now I prefer the term "midlife opportunity" as it implies that I can make choices and I am capable of moving to a better place. The awakening demanded I look at myself and allowed me to accept myself. This period of awakening brought forth an insatiable urge to learn about life. Now I am fully awake! My consciousness is alive and active, my options are in front of me, and I have the maturity to take action on my needs. I am ready to define myself on my own terms. I must be true to myself. I am ME! — Fran

When does midlife begin?

You can't tell if you've entered a midlife transition by counting the number of candles on your cake. Reaching a certain age that ends in zero is not as accurate a predictor of transition as experi-

Your Wake Up Call 9

encing your first jolt of awareness that time is passing. If you've purchased your first pair of reading glasses, plucked a dark chin hair, or watched your parents' health decline, you've already received your wake-up call.

A few years ago, just as her daughters were becoming more independent and needing her less, Carolyn's mother's health started to fail. Although her mother is in an assisted living facility with private duty nursing, it's still up to Carolyn to handle her finances and manage her care.

"My mother asked me recently, 'And just exactly when was it that we switched roles?' Sometimes it feels like everyone wants a piece of me! I need time for myself too," she said.

As you see age forty or fifty staring you in the face, you may begin to panic. This can create a sense of urgency — an insistent awareness that time is more important now than it ever was — and you don't want to waste it. After all, you have goals and aspirations yet to achieve.

While forty typically represents the beginning of midlife, stressful life events — death of a parent or family member, divorce, loss of job, career change, significant personal illness, or early onset of menopause — may initiate the transition process in some cases as early as your mid- to late-thirties. On the other hand, you may be in your fifties and believe you've successfully avoided the process completely simply because you've failed to recognize what's happened.

Kathy, age 47, was in her mid-thirties when she experienced a midlife transition. After ten years working as a manager at a Christian bookstore,

Kathy quit to start a family. "There was too much stress at work and I was having trouble getting pregnant," she explains. Her daughter, Cassie, was born a year later.

"It was a tough transition. Cassie was colicky for the first four months and I missed the accolades from work. Sometimes I questioned whether I'd made the right decision. I felt like I'd lost my identity. Also, my sister died shortly after Cassie was born. She had requested that Brian and I raise her three children, but her ex-husband showed up the day before her funeral and demanded his paternal rights to them. I felt like I'd lost my sister all over again. That weekend, we discovered we were expecting once more and Brad came into the picture. A year after he was born, however, my dad died and I went into severe postpartum depression. I felt like I'd never be 'normal' again. I was totally hopeless."

Wanting to protect herself from any more pain, Kathy withdrew; she ended up avoiding intimacy and blocking out the people that she loved the most. It especially affected her relationship with her husband.

An older woman from church befriended Kathy and renewed her hope. When Brad was six months old, she started doing some consulting work for another bookstore, which helped her during her transition. "I realized I needed to have an identity completely separate from my work or my role as a wife and mother.

"Since I got all that out of the way in my thirties, turning forty meant I finally had time for Brian again. For years, our marriage had been stagnant because I had nothing left to give him. We operated on a survival level because I was living in fear — fear of rejection, loss, and failure — rooted in losing my sister and my dad at such a transitional time in my life."

By the time her mom died three years ago, Kathy had learned to thank God for everything — even the trials. "Women like things secure and predictable, to be in control of our circumstances," Kathy says. "But God pushes us out of our comfort zone and expects us to live by faith."

Loss...we all encounter it in one form or another in our life. In midlife especially we lose things. Some lose their spouses, some lose their attachment to youth, and some lose things they believed in — whether it's religion or a way of looking at life. —Angie

Change is inevitable

As a mother of two teenagers and two other children knocking on the door of adolescence, I found myself reading numerous parenting books on how to help guide a child through these transition years. Certain characteristics echoed a familiar ring — identity crisis, moodiness, uncertainty, discontent, shifting roles, changing bodies — and I realized that what the authors were describing was very similar to the changes I was going through myself.

I began wondering, "Were there certain stages characteristic of all life transitions?" After talking to a number of other women and doing some research on my own, the answer came back a resounding, "Yes!"

Transition, according to Webster's Dictionary, is "a passage from one stage to another, whether gradual or abrupt." Transition by its very nature involves change, and change can be difficult. Change, even by choice, turns the familiar into the unfamiliar, resulting in feelings of fear and inadequacy as you enter unknown territory.

Midlife is a time for reevaluation and not just moving from one year to the next. If you use midlife as a time for readjusting your focus and a chance to start afresh, you'll reduce the apprehension that comes with passing forty and open your eyes to the opportunities that await you. Women who devoted their twenties and thirties to raising a family or pursuing a career, regard midlife as a new beginning.

For Paula, life became more meaningful when she came to the realization that she had less of it. "Trying to hang onto your youth is like trying to hold a fistful of sand," she said. "All we can do is acquire that new identity as we mature and ripen — and then we just run with it! You have to accomplish those dreams and goals because no one else is going to accomplish them for you.

"It's a matter of being at peace with yourself. Before you arrive at the peace, you have to experience the discomfort of acquiring that new identity. To acquire that new identity, we often have to lose a part of our old self which can be very difficult because most of us have become somewhat settled with the way things are."

Like adolescence, midlife transition is a period of getting a sense of who you are and establishing your identity. Midlife may be denied, but not escaped. It's a biological inevitability to grow and enter the next stage of development. Just as adolescence transforms you from a child to an adult, midlife transforms you from the person you think you are to the person you were meant to be. Midlife is a new birth, a new beginning, a chance to start over. It's a time to pursue your dreams and put yourself on the path to a fuller, more abundant life.

Wouldn't it be nice if our lives could be magically transformed without having to go through the awkward, and sometimes painful, process of transition? While that's not possible, gaining a clearer understanding of the transition process allows you to reduce your resistance to change and view it instead as an opportunity for growth.

This may seem like a difficult period in life, but really, wasn't it much worse to be a teenager? Remember when a pimple could stop the sun in its orbit and an insufficient smile from some kid on the football team could extinguish the stars? And isn't it better to actually know something, instead of just thinking that you do? —Roxanne

Understand the stages of transition

There are five distinct stages of transition.

1. The **AWARENESS** stage is when you finally confront your own mortality and the fleeting nature of life. You realize you won't live forever and you sense the urgency to experience life to its fullest. You're less willing to spend your time in a job that has no lasting value or in a relationship that is essentially unhealthy. You're more selective about the kind of people you allow into your life and have less time for petty concerns.

2. The **CRISIS** stage is a time when you are mourning a loss — a time for facing your emotions and putting the past behind you. Do you find yourself easily irritated or close to tears for no apparent reason? Be careful not to dismiss this as "just hormones." You may be grieving losses you aren't fully aware of yet. Old wounds may be resurfacing. You find yourself trying to take tighter control of your life in an attempt to avoid or deny the inevitable changes that are threatening to throw your life into a tailspin. Regrets or "what-ifs" might be haunting you.

3. The **SORTING OUT** stage is a time for personal reflection — an opportunity for exploring your options and asking questions: deep, introspective questions about your life. You experience frequent moments of insight and hunger for more time alone. You seek more meaningful friendships with people who can share your life

on an intimate level. This is likely to be the stage that will last the longest and be the hardest, yet the process will transform you if you trust it.

4. The **VISION** stage is where you begin to feel a renewed sense of energy and enthusiasm for life. You question yourself less — or at least for shorter periods. You desire to start something new: a project, a class, a career, or a relationship. You feel as if an inside voice is saying, "This is me!" If you use your insights drawn from the sorting out stage to formulate a new vision, you're ready for the action stage.

5. The **ACTION** stage is when you feel energized and grounded at the same time. You want to be out in the world, to be a part of something bigger than yourself. You find you have more fun now and play more than ever before. You know what you need to do to take care of yourself and you do it. You spend less time thinking about things and more time doing them. You feel a passion about almost everything you do; you feel fully engaged in your own life.

A transition is successfully completed when its lessons are clear, and the external events — as well as the inner turmoil — have calmed down, resulting in an inner peace and a new level of comfort with the woman who is emerging.

Out of the blue, I have become an emotional basket case! I start crying for no reason, I snap at people more often, and I suffer long periods of melancholy moods. I used to be so easy-going and carefree. What happened? Is that what it's all about? Doesn't it make you just a bit nuts? Like you want to shed everything and become someone new? New everything — new life, new surroundings, new identity — but then you wonder, 'Would this really make anything better?' Probably not. You just can't pinpoint what's wrong... because everything seems to be! Arrrghhh! Then you have those normal days when you wonder what your problem was in the first place. —Cara

I felt like life had passed me by and I had for-gotten to get on. I began to regret the choices I had made for my life. In a nutshell, I felt bewil-dered and lost. As a woman, I realized what was going on was part of the process of midlife, but was totally unprepared for how strong these feelings were. I began the process around age thirty-five and I would say it's been four years of intensive hell. I feel wonderful now in comparison. I am still learn-ing and growing...just not at such an "in your face" speed. —Julianne

For me, it was as though I woke up one day with the thought, "Hey, life is passing me by and I don't want to miss it." Before midlife, my attention was focused on others and the days just passed by in an endless parade of dishes, laundry, etc. As midlife appeared, it was with the realization that I was not happy with the choices I had made. It stopped me in my tracks! It made me look at life and myself in a different perspective. I was so drained emotionally that I was ready for change. The most important part of growth in midlife is the readiness for change. It will not force itself on you, but indirectly it is caused by the events of your life. —Sonya

I remember at 37 I started feeling unhappy with some of the choices I'd made. That was fifteen years ago and I still have some unresolved issues with that. Now I am mourning the extra weight gain and sore knees that come with getting older. I have felt especially dismal since my mother passed away. I was "young" until that happened. I believed I could always change things when I was ready. Now I am much more comfortable with myself, but I'm wondering if the quality of my life will go down hill quickly now. There is still so much I want to do. —Helene

There is a part of me that desires something else. Seems though that I get doing something that I think I want to be doing and I just don't enjoy it. I start longing to do something else. I am just never satisfied doing much of anything anymore. —Kim

I think midlife serves two purposes — to show us we are not as tough as we think we are and to prove to us that we in fact have a greater potential than we previously thought. My personal experience is that events trigger the midlife process — when we have become worn down emotionally by the demands of life and become trapped in our own web. I also believe hormones are partly responsible for the chaos we experience. I think midlife is a culmination of these two things. —Marlene

Trust the process

Midlife is a time of reflection and an opportunity to take an inventory of your life. One of the frequently asked questions is, "Are you happy with the direction your life is going?"

Prior to midlife, Jo was clearly not happy with the direction her life was taking. She was unfocused. Through the unfolding of midlife, she went from not knowing to knowing. The direction she chose became the best choice for her and those around her.

"It certainly became one of the most positive experiences of my life. I can say that I am much happier where life is leading me now than before," she said.

It's important to trust the process — especially during the sorting-out stage when your sense of confusion is at its peak — having faith that the answers will present themselves when you're ready.

Spend time in solitude and take time for the deep introspection needed to reflect on your life and explore the possibilities for the future. Learn to "stay in the question" and resist the tendency to make quick decisions in order to fill the void. By taking the time to investigate your options, you'll discover a wider range of choices, and you're more likely to find the best solution for you.

Explore a new activity — playing the guitar, backpacking, photography, learning to use a computer, quilting — and access parts of yourself that are yearning to be expressed. It might not turn out the way you planned, but the process is valuable because you'll build your self-confidence just knowing you dared to try something new!

Your challenge is to find ways to perform the critical inner work of exploring your thoughts and dreams, while continuing to carry on with your daily responsibilities. Basically, you must learn to run on two tracks at the same time. You must learn to live in a state of continual uncertainty until eventually one or two choices become clear as the next step to take and the vision stage begins.

I am thoroughly enjoying discovering myself. I am learning a lot about me — how I handle things, what motivates me, and how to take care of myself. Most of all, I am enjoying the process. A good friend once told me, "Enjoy the moment you are in, regardless of the circumstances." I think of that when I encounter unhappy moments, but I also remember it when the moments are happy. It goes along with being more aware of what is going on around me, experiencing all the emotions and not trying to hide from them or rush through them. —Claire

Learning about ourselves is a lifelong process so, as we grow older, we will continue learning about who we are. There are a lot of things I wish I could take back or do differently, but I wouldn't have learned from it and wouldn't have come to the place where I am now. —Louise

Action Steps:

1. Begin to chronicle your journey through midlife. Write down what you're experiencing and what's changing in your life. Journaling is a valuable tool for organizing your thoughts, evaluating new ideas, and tracking your progress. By documenting your feelings and insights, you will gain clarity and guidance for making major, life-altering decisions.

2. Ask yourself, "How can I change my views on midlife so that I embrace it instead of resisting it?"

3. Identify at least five life-altering experiences you've had in your life — both good and bad — and ask yourself how these turning points have influenced you.

4. Answer this question in your journal, "Have I sacrificed my dreams to achieve goals that have left me dissatisfied?" Write down any you can think of and then explore one dream more in-depth.

5. Form a group of Path Partners. A strong support system will help you put the ideas contained in this book into action. Our website, www.PathPartners.com, offers additional materials and guidelines for setting up your own Path Partners group.

CHAPTER TWO:
LETTING GO OF THE PAST

*"As women in midlife, we can look back and
see how even the difficult times in our lives
served a purpose in shaping the stronger and
more confident person that we've become.
We are who we are because of those
experiences, not despite them."*

—Sarah, Duchess of York

As a single parent, Maureen set her twelve-hour workday around her son Eric's schedule so she would be home when he was. Eric had swimming practice at 6 a.m. before school and again after school until 6 p.m. so she arranged her life accordingly, but as she approached her fortieth birthday, she was also approaching another milestone: Eric would be leaving for college and she would be living alone for the first time in her life.

"He's striving for more independence all the time, but I still try to consciously spend time with him every day. I feel like my time left with him is so limited," she said.

When change is forced on you by circumstances beyond your control, don't fall into the temptation to allow bitterness, anger, and fear to control your life. Instead, even in the face of devastating hardships, use this experience as a catalyst to stop and take stock.

An honest assessment of your life is the only way to determine any course corrections you might need to make. After all, where you are today is a direct result of the choices you have made in the past. The past, however, does not need to equal the future. Simply realize that you have to accept who you are today before you can transition successfully into the next stage of your life. Once you've taken stock of where you are and where you want to go, you'll feel more focused and energized.

In midlife I have tried to find my true self. Part of midlife is coming to grips with this true self. The hard part is watching the old self fade away. As our new self emerges, it sometimes screams to be heard. Our old, "false" self is still holding on, not wanting to relinquish control. Like a favorite pair of shoes that are too old to be comfortable anymore, we must discard the old self and continue to nurture the new self. We do this in steps — some small steps and some giant steps. —Darcy

Embrace your emotions...and release them!

Are you carrying around emotional baggage from your past? Is your life clouded by resentment, unforgiven hurts, perceived wrongs, and unacknowledged losses? Have you erected walls around your heart to keep from being hurt again?

If you're unable to express anger, sadness, grief, guilt, or hurt — if you suppress your emotions — you won't be able to move on. Unfortunately, denial of your feelings may cause unexpected outbursts or severe depression. You awake one day to realize that the walls you've so carefully built around you also keep you from enjoying life.

Part of midlife is openness to healing. We have shut out hurts for so long that we don't recognize them. Similar to stepping over the same box in the garage for years in a row, we just get used to it being there and habitually step over it while no longer "seeing" it. —Mimi

I believe it's important to accept and allow yourself to feel your feelings. Don't try to talk yourself out of being angry — express it and move on. —Sue

Make room for happiness in your life by resolving issues from the past. Forgive those who have "wronged" you. Refuse to hold any resentment. When you perpetuate hurt feelings and hold onto anger and bitterness, secret grudges, and revengeful feelings, you will eventually be poisoned by your own thoughts. Anger may seem justified, but is it worth it?

Maybe you need to return to the community where you grew up or a former place where you lived and put closure on some old relationships. Like Reese Witherspoon's character did in the movie *Sweet Home Alabama,* you might need to make peace with your past by seeing it in a new light.

It may seem foolish to turn the other cheek when you have been hurt. You may feel that releasing your negative thoughts or emotions will let the person who hurt you off the hook. You may even believe that holding onto hatred, bitterness, or hurt feelings is a way of punishing them. When you harbor deep emotions of pain and hostility, you give your power away to the very person who hurt you. They win the game every time you put your life on hold, every time you overwhelm yourself with sadness, every time you feel sorry for yourself.

So why would you want to hold onto your pain? Be aware that letting go of your anger takes away your alibis. As long as you hold onto the pain in your life, you have an excuse for why your life isn't the way you would like it to be. It's easier to blame others for your circumstances than to take responsibility for your own happiness.

If you really want to increase your happiness, you have to really want to let go of the pain. As long as there is part of you that wants to hang onto these negative thoughts and emotions, you will

never be free of them. If your pain is deep c
have been holding onto it for a long time, yo
to get to the point where you are so fed up
sick and tired of living your life like this — ...at
you're willing to let it go once and for all.

After Suzanne's husband left her unexpectedly
for another woman, she was filled with anger and
bitterness. Feeling that her life was over, she sank
into a deep depression. One day she realized that
her anger was only hurting herself, so she decided
to change her attitude. Whenever a negative
thought, emotion or memory popped into her head,
she would say to herself, *"Stop! I'm not letting this
control my life any longer! I am choosing to be happy
today — no matter what. I am a wonderful person
with a lot to offer. I will no longer accept anything
into my mind that tears me down."*

Suzanne's experiment worked. She started
seeing herself as a person who chose to be free from
the influence of negative thoughts and emotions so
she could enjoy life to the fullest. She chose to see
herself as a victor — not as a victim. Suzanne also
wrote her husband a letter explaining how his
actions had hurt her. She didn't need to mail the
letter; just expressing herself and the pain he had
caused allowed Suzanne to finally forgive him and
let it go.

Women especially have a tendency to keep themselves in an angry place by relating an account of
what happened over and over and over again in
hopes of gaining sympathy. Initially, it may be wise
to share your hurt with a close friend or professional counselor to gain perspective on the situation, but too many women beat the story to a pulp.

After a while, it's best to move on and let what happened in the past remain in the past.

Before midlife if I were feeling angry, I would unconsciously deny it because I considered anger to be immature. At midlife, however, I accept my anger as an honest feeling. I accept my emotions as a part of me that must be embraced and understood. For so many years I stuffed my feelings because I thought it was shameful to have them. It's a wonder I didn't explode! Today when a feeling comes along that makes me uncomfortable, I am learning to examine my feeling, find out what caused it, and what I can do about it. By going through this process, I am learning more about myself.
—Tanya

Not until my mid-thirties did I have a clue that I was somebody other than a wife and mother. Nor did I have a clue as to what I was feeling other than rage! Now I know that many of the mistakes I made in my earlier years weren't due to a character flaw as much as it was due to pain...deep, emotional pain! I need now to forgive myself and lay those burdens down. —Margaret

An exceptionally demanding responsibility for many women is caring for an aging parent. Trading roles with your parents is one of the most stressful situations you'll encounter. You face losing someone you can confide in, your sense of security, and may even miss an opportunity to vacation with friends or accept a long-awaited promotion.

The burden of coping with a parents' illness can potentially be an opportunity, however, for healing old rifts and discovering a deeper tenderness and affection in your relationship. Whatever the situation, it's critical that you have someone, or a group of people, who you can lean on for emotional support and who will provide you a safe haven for sharing your pain, frustrations and disappointments.

At forty, Cheri is finding herself dealing with her parents' medical needs. She recently became conservator of her parents' estate following her mother's diagnosis of cancer and a series of strokes that have taken out part of her father's ability to reason. Although she has three sisters, Cheri is the one that her mother calls when she's heard bad news from the doctor.

"Mom will say, "Honey, I'm calling you because I didn't want to ruin anyone else's day.' I jokingly say, 'Gee, thanks Mom!' but I really count it a privilege to spend this time with them. It's an honor to be able to help them and when I look back someday, I won't have any regrets. I'll know that I did what I could for them.

"I feel very motherly towards my parents these days. It's strange how our roles have reversed. Now Mom and Dad will 'tattle' on each other. It's really kind of childish. I'm trying to allow them some dignity though.

"Last week I cried at a funeral of someone I didn't even know because I was thinking of Mom's mortality. My family wasn't real 'touchy-feely' while I was growing up. Now I'm able to tell Mom, 'I love you' as I rub her legs during her painful chemo treatments.

"Dad hasn't exactly been the quintessential father. He was a good provider financially, but I couldn't relate to him emotionally. I've really only had a relationship with him in the last few years. Since the strokes, it's gotten even worse. He makes completely inappropriate comments and exhibits totally irrational behavior.

"It's been stressful, but it's helped me make decisions about how I want to manage my own life over the next thirty years. I've scaled back on work so I can spend more time at home with Scott."

Cheri and Scott have been together for eighteen years. She realizes that while taking care of her parents, she has to nurture her own relationship.

"A good marriage takes attention day in and day out. I realize now that my parents have been just existing. Scott is such a source of strength for me; I couldn't have gotten through this last year without him. He's my highest priority, and I really value my time with him."

Life gets more precious to me as I get older, especially after losing some family members and some dear friends. Living life to the fullest becomes my goal, not what I can possess by way of material things. —Lynne

There's something really sucky about having your parents go to a nursing home! I went to visit my father this evening and even though he is never coming home, he smiled and laughed a lot. It makes you wonder about life and the quality of it, especially at midlife, when there is such a change of emphasis. We give up so much of chasing the things we thought were so important and begin to reflect on more enduring things. —Sally

My understanding is that there are many of us at our age who are dealing with ill parents, which only exacerbates our own feelings of disappointment with life. The daily grind wears us down, especially upon witnessing the frailty of human life, causing many to question it altogether. It can be seen as a signal that all is not well within us. I think every time we face a disappointment, it is to open our eyes to ourselves and through the crisis learn that life goes nowhere by itself. For every loss we experience, there is something to be gained. Whether we lose our parents or a part of ourselves, we gain compassion, we gain understanding, and we ultimately gain growth as individuals. —Barbara

Witnessing the aging of my own parents and the sad, but necessary ending of their lives, I feel as though I've come face-to-face with my own mortality. At times, when I stop long enough to catch my breath, I feel so much sorrow. The death of my parents is by far one of the hardest things I've ever had to deal with. —Jill

After a long-term chronic illness, my mother passed away last year. While she was alive, I spent as many as four nights a week with her. I was her only connection to the world. She never learned the language and never made any friends. She was constantly depressed and relied on me to take care of her emotional needs. Since her death, I feel incredibly released. —Inge

Happiness is up to you

Martha Washington once said, "the greater part of our happiness or misery depends upon our dispositions, and not upon our circumstances."

In other words, thoughts are powerful; they can either help you or harm you. You may find yourself in a horrible situation, but it's not the situation causing your feelings of helplessness and despair;

it's what you think of the situation and how you respond to it. By focusing on the good things and being grateful for the positive aspects of your life, you can face any situation — no matter how devastating — and turn it into one of hope. You are not helpless. You are able to control your thoughts and thus determine the attitude with which you face your circumstances.

It is physically impossible to remain downhearted while you are acting out the symptoms of being radiantly happy. Dwelling on the bad things, when there is nothing you can do to change the situation, will only make you feel worse and will do absolutely no good. You can't always control what thoughts pop into your head, but you can control whether or not you dwell on them. You are the gatekeeper of your mind; don't give negative thoughts free reign.

Maybe you're plagued by guilt. We've all been there! It disrupts your inner peace, keeping you awake at night and leaving you with a knot in your stomach. When you think about what you have done and realize the full extent of your actions, you need to seek forgiveness and to make amends if possible. Then commit to avoiding such behavior in the future. Beyond this, stewing over it and rehashing the event endlessly will serve absolutely no useful purpose other than to rob you of your joy.

This is a quote that inspired me during a particularly difficult time in my life. *"Whatever life takes away from you — let it go. When you surrender and let go of the past, you allow yourself to be fully alive in the moment. Letting go of the past means that you can enjoy the dream that is happening right now."*

Are your "rules" for happiness making you miserable? Instead of clinging to a list of criteria that must be satisfied in order for you to experience happiness, celebrate each individual circumstance that makes you happy. For instance, appreciate one new outfit without needing to have an entire new wardrobe to be happy. Enjoy one new piece of furniture without having to replace all the furniture in the house, or even in a single room. Acknowledge an effort on the part of your teenage son or daughter to help around the house without lamenting all the other routine chores you wish they'd do. Don't insist, "I have to make everyone happy." Be satisfied that you have friends who love and appreciate you. You don't need to please everybody all of the time. Living like this makes it so much simpler and easier to be happy and content.

Your search for fulfillment and happiness will remain elusive as long as you go on looking outside of yourself. Husbands, children, and work will continue to disappoint you if you expect them to make you feel complete and satisfied. You have to search within.

I am exploring who I am, rediscovering myself, wanting desperately to accept all my feelings, reexamine my sexual self, reflect on my past and try to accept what I did, and in certain cases trying to forgive myself for all I did not do. —Donna

My midlife passage right now is the transition from fulltime mother to whatever I am going to do for the rest of my life. I would like to have a career, but sometimes I feel too weary to imagine starting out in the business world. I am finding that I am developing a sense of selfishness as I go deeper into midlife. I have no guilt. I know my kids are older now, and I can afford the luxury, but I am focusing much more on me. I alternate between supreme confidence and "what the heck am I doing?" I look at my fifteen-year-old daughter with love one day, and the next day she cuts me to the bone. I find myself wondering, "What I was thinking, staying home all those years and letting life pass me by?" —Beth

Learn from your mistakes and move on

Sometimes things don't go the way you originally planned. You forget to pay a bill, make a social blunder, or go on an eating binge and gain ten pounds. Accept that setbacks will occur and keep them in perspective. When you make a mistake, ask yourself: "How can I learn from this?" By treating your mistakes as learning experiences instead of disasters or failures, you put yourself in a state of mind that allows you to find a solution, forgive yourself and move on.

Observe children. They fall and get up and try again and again until they finally learn to walk.

35

laugh at themselves. They are immensely .ous and constantly trying new things. And ey sleep soundly without replaying all the little blunders they made that day.

Maybe children understand instinctively that beating yourself up over mistakes is a perfect way to destroy your motivation and discourage yourself from trying again. What can you learn from them? Keep trying until you finally succeed. Learn to laugh at yourself. Maintain your sense of wonder and be willing to take risks. Build yourself up instead of tearing yourself down. Self-criticism will cripple you emotionally far worse than anyone else's opinion. If you don't love yourself unconditionally, you can't truly love others.

Stop playing the victim

Life doesn't always turn out as you imagined it would. I know a guy who experienced the following: a child born mentally impaired, a serious car accident which left him in chronic pain, a wife who had an affair and left him with a young child to raise, the loss of his mother to cancer, and the depletion of his life savings in a downturn of the stock market. Is he a victim? The answer lies in how you look at life.

Victims let circumstances determine how they feel. When something happens, their attitude is, "It's their fault," "They did this to me," "I'm going to get them for this!" Well, stop whining and feeling sorry for yourself! When you complain and wallow in self-pity, your focus is on what's wrong with your life. Think instead about what's good about your life right now and start living in gratitude for all you

have been blessed with! Focus on the positive —
not the negative!!

*What you feed your brain comes about. If
you're always dwelling on what's wrong, that's
what you manifest in your life. For instance, I
started menopause around age 35. I became
depressed and "weepy" because I couldn't get
pregnant again. Then I decided to be grateful
for the little seven-year-old daughter I already
had. Now she's a grown woman, working as a
teacher. We're still very close. —Joyce*

Refuse to blame

At 44, Carol is happy and content with her life.
But it wasn't always this way. Married young, she
spent her twenties and thirties raising her four
children (now ranging in age from 16 to 22). Her
dream had been to live in a big city and work in the
field of writing and publishing. Instead, she chose
to be a stay-at-home mom. "It was hardest when
my second child was born — no big city, no writing
and publishing career — just the prospect of more
babies," says Carol. "I thought to myself, 'What did
I get myself into?'"

She worked hard at her role of mother. "I put my
heart and soul into those kids," says Carol proudly.
"I wouldn't go back and change it, but it sure wasn't
easy back then. I was just living day-by-day. I
couldn't see the big picture. I didn't feel like I had
any options. I thought, 'What else could I do?' At

thirty-nine, I finally decided to separate from this path that had been chosen for me and started making my own choices."

One of the first changes Carol made in her life was the decision to lose the excess weight she'd put on during her four pregnancies and the years of staying home with her children. She joined a health club and signed up for Weight Watchers, losing 45 pounds that she has successfully kept off for five years. She works out daily.

"I'm fanatical about exercise!" claims Carol. "I do yoga, cardio and weight training at the health club and about a year ago, I started running. Several mornings a week, I run three to five miles near my home. It's a wonderful meditative time for me and I feel really good when I'm able to begin my day with a run."

Motivated by her newfound energy, Carol went back to school for her doctorate degree and started teaching. She has been teaching eighth grade for several years and loves it.

"Becoming a teacher definitely stretched my comfort zone," admits Carol. "There's not a single teacher in my entire family. They're all professional people, dressed in nice clothes and working in air-conditioned offices. Teaching sure has turned out to be a better career than what I thought it would be. It demands a lot more of me both creatively as well as intellectually." Her current goal is to begin teaching college level education courses.

Carol has also found time to travel. In addition to two cruises she's taken with her daughter, she's traveled throughout the United States and journeyed to Hong Kong and Israel. Next summer, she plans to visit her daughter in Italy.

"I lived a false identity for a long time," observes Carol. "It's only been in the past five years that I really decided who I was and what I wanted to do with my life. When I was in my twenties and thirties, I didn't feel like I had a lot of options; turning forty has offered hope!"

Don't blame other people and circumstances if you don't have the kind of life you think you deserve. Blaming serves only one purpose — making you feel like a victim. And a victim doesn't have power over her own life. Someone with a victim mentality thinks life happens to her; she remains helpless. She's not involved in creating her own experience. She looks at her circumstances and asks the question, "Why me?" She'll blame her situation — not having enough money, a dead-end job, unsupportive parents, or the demands of children — and use it as her excuse for not pursuing her dreams.

Don't expect your friends to make you happy. Stop waiting for your partner to motivate you to reach your goals. You need to look within yourself. You have to believe that you have what it takes. One of my husband's favorite sayings is "If it's to be, it's up to me." See what you can create when you set your mind and energy in a positive direction. You are the one responsible for the outcome of your life. You can't change your past, but you can create your future. It's not too late!

Many women don't bother making something of their lives because they believe they're destined to fail. Unfortunately, this becomes a self-fulfilling prophecy. You need to understand that you can only control yourself. You can't control the weather, other drivers on the road, your kids or spouse, or anything outside of your own beliefs, thoughts, and actions. If other people are the problem, you think you have to change them, but if you take responsibility for your life, then you only have to change you. Society has become so focused on women as victims that we fail to see our choices and options.

According to an old Chinese proverb, "The gem cannot be polished without friction, nor man perfected without trials." Imagine how boring life would be if it was always smooth sailing on the sea of life! Stories would never have a plot because there would never be any challenges to overcome. Adversity spices life up a little! Every hardship or difficulty you encounter refines your character and shapes you inwardly.

"Everything that comes into my life helps me grow," says Diane. "If I accept it and don't fight it, it doesn't become a challenge, but rather an asset in my life."

Following a crisis, you become a stronger person — able to influence and inspire those around you to improve their lives as well as your own.

Choose to break bad habits

Luanne's fortieth birthday was a turning point in her life.

"It was then that I came to the realization that I was just surviving life by anesthetizing myself with alcohol," admits Luanne, now fifty. "My husband at the time told me, 'I'd rather have you as an alcoholic, and not have to talk to you.' It was time to reevaluate what I needed to do and make some changes.

"Acknowledging my fears opened up a whole new life for me. Living sober meant stepping out into virgin territory. I gave up everything except my life. I actually gained my life and I'm a much better person for it, but it was very frightening."

What habits are holding you back? Your everyday normal behavior has a lot to do with the results in your life. If you're not happy with these results, something has to change.

Many of our daily activities are simply routines. From the time you get up until you go to bed, there are hundreds of activities that you do the same way every day. If you want to effectively change some aspect of your life, you need to alter your behavior. Start identifying the habits, attitudes and thinking that need to change — little behaviors and thought patterns that are holding you back — instead of doing the same thing over and over again and expecting different results.

Choose to break a bad habit. Take the biggie first. If you don't know what it is, ask a friend — someone who will be honest with you. Focus every effort on breaking that habit — stop smoking, get out of debt, lose your excess weight, put your house in order — whatever it is, tackle it head on!

Marla Cilley, better known as the FlyLady, has revolutionized habits and routines for women — and probably a few men that frequent her website out of curiosity! She tells her faithful followers (known as "FlyBabies") to make their beds every morning, check their laundry, shine their sinks, and get dressed (seems obvious, but when you're in the throes of depression, daily dressing can be a chore).

Marla now has women all over the globe cleaning

their bathrooms and starting a load of laundry before heading out the door in the morning. And her loyal FlyBabies wouldn't dream of hitting the hay at night without shining their kitchen sinks and decluttering all their "hot spots!"

Motivational speaker, Jim Rohn, talks about the principle of the "Slight Edge." He recommends you periodically ask yourself, *"What small but steady activities can I be doing today, that over a long period of time can lead to big, long-term results?"* And conversely, *"Am I neglecting to do any of the very easy, doable basics that can make a major difference in my future?"* Once you create a clear image of the rewards and benefits this new habit will give you, you'll feel more focused and energized.

The secret is not slipping back into past behaviors. Don't resort to the old, familiar ways of doing things simply because it's easier than sticking with your new habits. Whenever you decide to eliminate bad habits, there's always an adjustment period. Eventually, the benefits of your new lifestyle will become apparent and they will outweigh any sacrifices you've had to make along the way.

About fifteen years ago, I was focusing all my time and attention towards others in the home or family because it took the focus off of me and my character defects that I had yet to work on. As long as I could stay busy, I didn't have to deal with what I needed to change in me. —Liz

Eliminate what you've been tolerating in your life

My friend Leslie has a car door handle that broke off when her vehicle went through the carwash. To make matters worse, her car only unlocks from the driver's side. To get into her car requires her to unlock it from the driver's side and then walk around to the passenger's side and slide across. She has been tolerating this situation for months. We laugh about it, but some irritations aren't that insignificant.

Women tolerate bosses who harass them and take advantage of them. They put up with abusive marriages. They succumb to the demands of their children. Maybe it's an adult son who is living at home, not going to school, not working, and not contributing to the household financially or physically. He stays out all hours of the night with his friends and then sleeps most of the day, leaving you with dirty laundry and a hefty grocery bill. You tolerate this situation because you're afraid of what might happen to him if you were to ask him to contribute or leave, but you're actually doing him a disfavor. You need to set some boundaries for yourself. You need to respect yourself and love him enough to make him start taking responsibility for his life.

If you are highly stressed at work, dislike or even hate your job, then I would encourage you to do some soul-searching. If you hate your job, then you shouldn't be there, period. If your job is very stressful, then you need to discover how to manage or eliminate that stress, or get a different job. I don't care how much money you make or the position that you hold — your health is more important than your job.

Has it ever crossed your mind to try a job very different from the one you have now? Don't automatically dismiss the thought as impractical or crazy. Often a dramatic career change can increase your satisfaction with life, reduce your stress, and even yield financial rewards in ways beyond your wildest imagination.

Tricia, age 57, worked as a pharmaceutical rep for seventeen years. Then, about fifteen years ago, she became disenchanted with her work. "I disdained the corporate mindset," says Tricia. "I would attend national conventions and they were so full of materialistic, artificial crap. I knew I needed to change course, but I was a single mother and the money was good. Then I read *In Search of Excellence* by Tom Peters, and it completely changed my perspective on life and work. I had to make some changes!

"Initially, I took a job with a different company, but after two years, I realized I'd just changed the scenery; the story was the same. I took a sabbatical to do a lot of internal cleansing. I needed to completely 'detox' and try something different."

Today Tricia is a homeopathic clinician in private practice. "I love what I'm doing! It fits me perfectly," she claims. "I've always been focused on health. This is a natural, holistic way to help other people improve their health. Someday I might try running a bed & breakfast in some exotic place like France or Italy, but for right now I'm exactly where I'm supposed to be."

Every day more women are taking the plunge. The prod may come from a layoff, burnout, or hitting the glass ceiling. Sometimes family issues drive the change. One woman left a lucrative career as a corporate tax attorney and pursued her passion by becoming a children's portrait photographer. Risky? Absolutely! But she loves every minute of it.

Financial security is a key component of an enjoyable, rewarding life. Work, however, is much more than generating income and providing for creature comforts. Your job occupies the majority of your waking hours. If you've just been putting in your time — feeling unfulfilled and indifferent toward your work — it may be time to switch to something different. If you're not happy about what you're doing, then you need to figure out why. Generally, it's not the boring routine that causes burnout, but a lack of passion and purpose in your work.

If you don't want to be where you are now, and you want your life to be something other than this, your only true option is to make some changes. Change takes courage, especially if you are feeling safe and secure the way things are. Change takes risk.

Identify small things, little behaviors that you would like to change in your life — tiny things that are holding you back. Once you've tackled the small changes, you'll find that bigger changes don't seem too insurmountable. FlyLady advises to start with shining your sink so you're not overwhelmed with the task of putting your whole house in order. What's the "shining sink" in your life?

What's bothering you?

At age 45, Shirley is a successful business owner, but it wasn't always that way. Coming from a family of seventeen children (ten sisters and six brothers), Shirley grew up very poor.

"I don't blame my parents for the decisions they made," says Shirley. "You can't change the past, only the future. Landing on my feet was my only choice. I simply refused to fail."

Married with a young daughter, Shirley was content. "We were a very happy, close-knit family. I loved raising Jamie, but I wanted to get her away from the negative influences of her aunts, uncles, and cousins. So when Jamie was two and a half years old, we decided to move to Texas — as far away from my childhood home as we could get."

Because she wanted to be a stay-at-home mom, Shirley ran a daycare until Jamie was in first grade. When Jamie started school, Shirley took a secretarial job at a computer company and cut back to part-time in the summers so she could be home with Jamie.

"I really wanted to give her opportunities that I never had growing up. Today she is married and works as a police officer in Chicago. She hopes someday to become a detective or join the FBI — and she'll do it, too!" Shirley said.

As Jamie started growing up and gaining some independence, Shirley knew it was time to start doing some things for herself. So when her daughter went to college, Shirley started taking classes. She wanted to try new things and meet new people, but she found she was intimidated by social situations.

"My old boss took me on sales calls and exposed me to new situations. I would say to myself, 'Oh, my gosh! I talked to a male person in a suit!' Then I started taking Dale Carnegie classes and reading self-help books. I got my ears pierced for the first time and started wearing make-up.

"Everything is about attitude; I eventually realized that people are just people. I still get nervous sometimes, but the anxiety goes away a lot quicker. Stepping out of my comfort zone has given me wonderful opportunities for growth."

Her husband of twenty-three years apparently wasn't happy with the changes in Shirley.

"The more I started coming out of my shell, the more he was threatened and tried to pull me back. I never realized what a controlling, possessive type guy he was," Shirley says. "I tried to involve him in my new life, but he resisted. He couldn't handle it that I was no longer accountable to him for everything. Soon the marriage crumbled. We went to marriage counseling for a while. I suggested a trial separation, but he wanted to make it final. Our marriage shouldn't have failed, but he was unwilling to compromise. I thought it was childish the way he handled it. He has big regrets now, but they're not my problem.

Suddenly single at forty-two, Shirley wondered, "What am I going to do with my life?" She realized it was just another opportunity to figure out how to succeed.

"I remember spending a night in a hotel room all by myself for the first time and thinking, *'If other people can do this, so can I.'*"

Shirley met John at a trade show; it was like talking to an old friend. They fell in love; she quit her job, bought a new car, and moved to Hawaii for almost a year. But after seven months, she came home very ill. She was immediately hospitalized and underwent a hysterectomy and gall bladder surgery. Shirley regained her health, and a year ago she started her own business.

"If somebody would have told me before that quiet, shy little Shirley would someday make presentations in front of a hundred people, I'd have said, 'No way!' Now, however, I see life as a challenge and I embrace it. I still have more growing to do, but I really like this new me!"

Women today are experiencing the need to start managing their own money and create some security for themselves. Because women's work histories are often erratic due to years of parenting responsibilities, it's not uncommon for midlife women to lack sufficient financial resources. If you've always relied on someone else to control your assets, it's time for you to become more financially savvy and start exercising your voice regarding important financial decisions impacting your future. Even if you hold funds jointly with your husband, you need to be involved in how the money is being spent and invested.

So, what's been bothering you lately? Attack the thing that is bothering you the most. Stop reacting to life and start taking control of what gets your time and attention. Set new priorities that reflect what's really important to you.

Action Steps:

1. Write down all the reasons why you want to make a change in your life and how this change will positively impact you. What will your life be like if you don't make this change?

2. If you are in the middle of some adversity right now, what resources are you drawing on? Who are you drawing closer to and working with? What part of your character is being tested and strengthened? What can you do to view this adversity as someone who will be better for it on the other side?

3. Gratitude is like a muscle. The more you use it, the stronger it gets. It's a choice...in every moment. Every day for twenty-one days, express gratitude and appreciation to one or more people (via email, phone, notes or cards, or in person). While you're engaged in acknowledging and expressing your gratitude, notice how it makes you feel. Don't do it, however, with the expectation that the other person must respond in kind. This is about what feeling and expressing gratitude does for you.

4. Give yourself some credit for what you have accomplished. Make a list — no achievement is too small or insignificant. You've probably come a long way! Acknowledge yourself. Congratulate yourself. Even reward yourself. Be grateful.

5. Jot down any blocking phrases that might be causing inner conflict. When one appears, simply note it, and replace it with an affirmation such as "I can," "Life is wonderful," "It feels great to share my gifts," "I'm loveable and capable," or "I have all that I need." Now you're changing your self-talk to empowering thoughts instead of disabling ones.

CHAPTER THREE:
EXPLORE NEW HORIZONS

"Pity the man who has a favorite restaurant,
but not a favorite author. He's picked out a
favorite place to feed his body, but he doesn't
have a favorite place to feed his mind!"

—*Jim Rohn*

Discover your passion — what excites you?

At age 35, Karen has discovered her passion – art!

"Everything I've done has led to this point in my life," says Karen. "I went to college despite my parent's disapproval and strong desire for me to settle down right away and get married. Later, I pursued my Master's degree in social work so I could become a licensed therapist. I think they were mortified!"

After finally reaching her goal of being a therapist in private practice, Karen realized she was completely disillusioned. She decided to take an oil painting class and suddenly became conscious of how much she enjoyed art! This led her to teaching an art therapy group for female cancer patients which they found rewarding and she discovered to be immensely satisfying.

During this time, a coffee shop owner in her neighborhood was moving and needed someone to take over his lease. "I had thought it would be nice to have my work in a gallery someday," explains Karen, "but slowly the vision for my own gallery began to take shape."

Six months ago, she opened her gallery in the former coffee shop space. It serves as a gallery, her private art studio, and a meeting place for her private and group therapy sessions. "I meet clients and host workshops on Monday and Tuesday and the gallery is open to the public Wednesday through Saturday.

"I've been able to combine all of my passions by dreaming outside the box," says Karen. "I feel so free being able to express who I truly am as a person without anyone trying to tell me, 'You need to be this way or that way.' I hate being restricted by those kinds of boundaries. I am able to be completely myself and be okay with it."

Like Karen, you can create space in your life for greater self-expression and creativity — passionate pursuits in which you get lost in what you really love. What excites you so much that you can't wait to get out of bed in the morning?

You may have thought your secret wish to write a children's book or learn country dancing was silly and pushed it to the back recesses of your mind. It may be that you want to learn how to play the guitar, take a pottery class, or write your own screenplay. Most of us have something that we have always wanted to do, or have a talent for.

Maybe you daydream about hiking in the woods and sketching in a nature journal or maybe you have always wanted to learn Italian. Revisit the activities you enjoyed as a child — playing the flute, bike riding, canoeing, ice skating, skiing — all the things you used to love, but as an adult, never felt you had time for.

Is there something you've thought about doing, but never thought you'd be capable of trying? Whether it's running a marathon, horseback riding, or becoming a clown, call on your courage and take the first step. Make the phone call, schedule the lesson, buy the supplies — whatever steps are required to convince your subconscious that you are serious about focusing on that goal. Stop making excuses!

There is no greater tragedy than to find yourself at the end of your life regretting that you never dared to explore your true passions. When you're doing what you love, your work improves, you're more productive, and you have more energy to direct toward other areas of your life. Pursuing what you enjoy inspires and renews you. It makes you feel alive. Your happy

Make a commitment to lifelong learning

A common thread I've discovered among the women I've interviewed is their commitment to growth and receptivity to new ideas. They never tire of learning, whether pursuing classes, reading or attending seminars. Women who have embraced midlife are constantly striving to improve themselves.

..., self-assured woman, Inge decided last ...ursue training as a lay speaker in the ...ethodist Church.

...n't fully understand what lies ahead for me, ...dmits Inge, "but I love being involved in ministry. For years, I've volunteered as a youth leader, chaired an administrative board and sat on the church finance committee. I also enjoy singing in our church's musical programs."

Inge, a treasurer for a worldwide service organization that feeds the hungry, helped her local chapter raise $28,000 for hunger relief this year. "I'm easily bored, so I try to stay occupied. I'm an avid reader," says Inge. "I typically have four to five books going at the same time."

We all need to find ways to continue to learn and grow. From birth until we reach adulthood, our learning curve is dramatic. We learn a tremendous amount very quickly — language, culture, history, science, mathematics. What our minds absorb during the first two decades of our lives is staggering.

For most women this accelerated learning curve levels off after they finish their formal education. With no more exams to take and no papers to write, there's no external motivation to read and study any more books. Imagine for a moment, however, what would happen if you kept up an accelerated learning curve the rest of your life? Can you imagine what you could learn to do, the skills you could develop?

Community colleges, universities, and community education centers offer adult courses on nights and weekends that can work around your busy schedule. But you can also open your mind to new ideas without taking classes. Sometimes the easiest way to learn is just by opening a book. Audiotapes, videos, and computer software also offer an opportunity to learn additional skills, acquire new knowledge, and increase your awareness of the world around you.

Midlife is a great time to go back to school and get a degree or pursue a dream you may have abandoned or deferred. I was inspired by one woman I spoke with who had committed herself to studying one subject in-depth every year. Continuing your education, whether taking a class or studying independently through books or tapes, invigorates more than your mind; it reawakens your connection to the world, adds to your bank of wisdom, and expands your horizons.

Libby, age 50, comes from a very large, unconventional family.

"There were ten of us kids and my mother, an artist, would move all the furniture out of the living room to make room for shuffleboard and a ping-pong table to keep us at home," she said. Attending an affluent high school, however, she discovered how cruel other kids could be. She didn't relate to them and their value system. She placated everyone in order to get along and avoided saying anything controversial so she wouldn't get picked on.

"It was very depleting! I vowed after that never to compromise again — to always be true to myself and embrace my individuality. Today I'm very comfortable with who I am. I'm my own best friend," she said.

Libby's goal is to keep evolving so she becomes more interesting and worth spending time with.

"I want to feel continually alive, not stale! People get into these horrible routines and become very dull. They simply don't stop to reevaluate what they want to be doing with their lives. They don't take time to refresh themselves and entertain the thought of a new career or new ways to spend their time and energy. I've always had a great zest for life. I can't imagine wasting a single day!"

An avid reader, Libby enjoys reading biographies, travel journals, and books on holistic health. "My favorite biographies are of individuals who were able to live as they wanted and had fascinating lives as a result," says Libby. "I also like reading about other places." Her own travels have taken her to Istanbul, Morocco, Spain, Italy, and France.

"I'm not really into chasing after a lot of material things, yet I'm able to live the lifestyle I choose." Libby funds her personal dreams by taking on freelance marketing projects and working part-time in a little vintage store with an upscale 'SoHo' feel to it. This combination works well to meet her needs.

"We live a very rich life, but we don't live in a big house. I don't think people really reflect on how they spend their money. If you just cut out some of the things you don't really need, you have the resources to do what's really important to you."

One of the priorities Libby makes time for in her life is taking classes at the local community college. Currently, she's taking a cultural geography course and has discovered that it's sparked an interest in her.

"My five-year game plan is to get my anthropology degree and do fieldwork in Africa. My two oldest children will be through with college by then and functioning in society. In June I'm taking a trip to France with a childhood friend. Next year I'm planning to move to Italy for a month, then a whole summer, and then a whole year. I'm also training for a triathlon. I just keep putting more carrots in front of myself!"

Libby believes that every woman has time to do what she wants to do. It just may mean rearranging her daily habits and schedule so that her use of time actually reflects her true priorities.

"I choose to get up at five o'clock in the morning so I have time to run, drink a cup of tea, and meditate. I really scrutinize how I spend my time so I have the flexibility to weed in my garden or read a good book.

"Although I have my vision and my goals, I also try to stay flexible and open to the experiences that refine who I am. People should have a whole list of remarkable things about them — what they've done and what they've experienced. I want all my years to be remarkable! I am continually sculpting myself into the person I want to be. I hope I can look back someday and think what a hysterically fun life I've led."

Strive to be a lifelong learner. Be the kind of woman who is determined to keep up her learning. Continue to read, take classes, attend seminars, as well as meet and talk to interesting people. Keep growing and trying new things. Growth is an enemy of old age. The woman who continues to expand her mind does not age nearly as rapidly as the one who has ceased to grow. Age begins when growth stops.

Most of us use only a small percentage of our capabilities, yet we can do so much more. You can utilize more of your own capacities by enrolling in a writing workshop, sculpting class, dance class, jewelry design, or a cooking class. Sue signed up to take piano lessons along with her teenage daughter and discovered she really enjoyed music. "I never thought I was musical before, but now I'd love to take singing lessons too." It's also never too late to learn a foreign language. You can pick up some tapes and learn in your car as you drive. Learning opens up whole new worlds!

Learning new things gives you a feeling of achievement. Reading books increases your knowledge of things in life and teaches you new skills or improves existing ones. Do something different from what you do all day at work. In undertaking a new after-hours project, start with something small and complete it, so as not to get discouraged. You will get a feeling of achievement when it is done.

People aren't old until their interest in life has left them. Choose to grow personally. Make a decision today to be a person who is on the never-ending journey of personal growth.

Develop the habit of reading daily

One way to feed your mind is through the writings of influential people. Maybe you can't meet the person, but you can read his or her books. People from all walks of life, people with incredible life experiences, people who have gone from failure to success have taken the time to write down their experiences to inspire and teach you.

Throughout my life, I have turned to books to teach myself something new. I homeschooled my children for ten years, and one of the advantages of teaching my children at home has been learning so many things I never learned (or appreciated) when I was going through my own formal education. I've explored ancient Rome, discovered owl behavior, and gained a new appreciation for the sacrifices made by America's founding fathers.

How many books have you read in the last three months? Reading books could enable you to develop your hobbies, enhance your relationships, further your knowledge, advance your career, improve your health, and expand your mind. So why then do so many people avoid reading the books that could enrich their lives? With literally thousands of books on library shelves waiting to be read, libraries offer you a buffet of intellectual feasting.

Those who wish for a better life cannot permit themselves to miss the books that could have a major impact on their lives. I remember years ago hearing Zig Ziglar reveal that he reads two to three hours a day! A little reading each day will result in a wealth of valuable information in a very short period of time. Feed your mind just as you feed your body. In ten years you will be the same person you are today except for the books you have read and the lives you have touched.

Understand the value of an hour

There are 525,600 minutes in every year; how do you want to spend them? Assuming one-third of those minutes are spent sleeping, you still have 346,896 minutes left to spend however you choose. Do you want to just let the days happen to you or do you want to plan?

Jolene felt as if she were drowning in a sea of everyone else's needs. It seemed that she was not even noticed as a person who had needs and feelings of her own. She felt as if she had lost her identity.

She purchased a digital camera and began to take photographs of nature. She then digitally added inspirational verses and turned her pictures into calendars, daily planners, wall art, and greeting cards. She entered a photography exhibit and, much to her surprise, sold several pieces. She sold even more at the next show and that encouraged her to keep going.

"I learned that giving up what you think you want, for the most part gives you back so much more. I feel good about myself now. I no longer feel as though I am just wandering through life, but have something valuable to contribute," she said.

"I am happiest when I am taking pictures and turning them into products that will bless other people. My children are happier, my husband is happier, and bottom line…I am happier with who I am and what I am doing with my life!"

Jolene's accomplishments in her photography help build her up to accomplish other goals in her life.

"I have finally gotten to a point that although I am still a wife and mother, I am also my own individual. Now I am taking time out for myself and getting to know me again.

"My photography is what keeps me alive in the middle of all this turmoil. It's my oasis. It keeps me producing something that is positive. It gives me a sense of accomplishment while everything else is so uncertain. It's mine!"

It's incorrect to say that you don't have enough time. It's how you spend your time that's important. Watching too much television can be a complete waste of time unless you're learning something in the process. If you're broadening your horizons, then yes, it's useful. Otherwise, you're better off reading a book that will open your eyes to a whole new world of ideas!

If you invest one hour each day in learning a new subject, you will accumulate nine 40-hour weeks over the course of a year. Imagine for a minute, how good you would become at something if you did it all day, every day for just over two months? Just 60 minutes a day may be the defining edge you need to really get the results you want from life.

How important is your time to you? What value do you place on your free time? Outside of sleeping, eating, household chores and other activities to sustain your life, what do you do with your time? How do you spend your "non-working" moments each day?

It is easy to lose sight of where your time goes. An hour here and an hour there may seem harmless enough. However, all of those hours add up to make a significant portion of your life. The average American spends more than four hours a day watching TV. Multiply that by fifty years and you have eight years spent staring at a box.

Ideally we should spend our time on the activities that are the most important to us — activities that will enrich our lives and the lives of those around us. But sometimes you get off track and need to readjust your priorities. You need to make sure that you're investing your time where it matters most.

If you find that you have been spending too much time on activities that aren't improving the quality of your life, don't worry about it; just decide that today will be your new beginning. A truly abundant life is not dependent upon luck or circumstance, but rather on how you spend your time. Spend it wisely.

If midlife is the second adolescence, then it is time to experiment. Just as in your youth, this is the time to stretch yourself by trying new things. So relax and enjoy trying new places, new people, and new ideas. It is the exploration that is important. We are reshaping our vision of ourselves and now is the time and place to see what we like and what fits our updated personality. —Gretchen

Someday I'd like to meet a guy who has a hobby or interest in common with mine, but you learn that if you want to do certain things, you just do them and don't wait for someone else; I have to do what I need to do to be happy. —Nell

When Eric is visiting his dad, I keep myself busy with home improvement projects — painting, wallpaper, and landscaping. I love to work on my house! I learned years ago that I didn't need a man around the house to get things done. It started out of necessity, but now I really enjoy it. I've always wanted to learn to play the piano, so I started taking lessons a month ago. Last winter, I took ice skating lessons. I was in class with a bunch of teenage girls, but we had a lot of fun! —Maureen

Action Steps:

1. Take time to expand your knowledge. Develop the habit of reading at least 20-30 minutes a day. Read something stimulating, challenging or which gives you an edge in your profession.

2. Pick one area of your life that you want to improve and commit the next 90 days to that one thing.

3. Imagine that a fairy godmother has given you the opportunity to do anything you want for the next year of your life. What would you choose to do?

4. What do you need to ignite the passion in your life — to bring back your childlike sense of wonder? Is it paints? A camera? Inline skates? Whatever it is, don't put off any longer getting in touch with the child inside of you.

5. Write down all of the things that you will do with your "free time" tomorrow. Then prioritize the list so that the most important activities are done first.

CHAPTER FOUR:
NURTURE YOUR MIND,
BODY & SPIRIT

*"It's good to have money and the
things money can buy, but it's good,
too, to make sure you haven't lost the
things that money can't buy."*
—George Horace Lorimer

Women need to learn to pamper themselves by indulging in activities that cause them to slow down and nurture themselves — in mind, in body, and in spirit. The benefits are immeasurable. By regularly carving out time for personal renewal, you will become less needy and less stressed out. You will replenish your energy and later be able to tackle your to-do-list with renewed enthusiasm. Most importantly, you will begin to feel special and send a confident message about yourself into the world.

I was very selfish during my midlife crisis. I had neglected myself for so long that it seemed I could no longer breathe at times. Sometimes it is necessary to be self-centered. I am much more of a giving person now because of the huge changes that took place in my life. I never would have gotten to this point, however, if I'd continued to ignore my needs and live in denial. —Aimee

Midlife changes the way we view our own bodies. The passing of time can be seen in our faces. We are better able, however, to change the way we approach our physical health. We need to come back to our bodies as we start our journey into the second half of life. We become better at listening to our own senses and have the maturity to act on becoming more aware of our own physical needs. —Lauren

Learn to relax — life isn't a race!

For Lisa, turning forty meant becoming a mother for the first time.

"Waiting until I was thirty-nine to get married allowed me time to find myself. I had plenty of opportunity to explore who I was without the added roles of wife and mother."

Her biggest challenge was starting her own business. She went from sales to suddenly being responsible for other people — managing a staff and paying their wages. Initially motivated by not wanting to let others down, Lisa discovered a lot of freedom in being able to make her own decisions and create her own destiny.

"Being a business owner has given me a lot of self-esteem, knowing I could be financially successful and support myself," she says. "I used to be a classic Type A personality, but I just don't get revved up about work anymore. Now the highlight of my day is spending time with my husband and my two-year-old son, Parker. It's nice after all these years to have a family to come home to."

Most women admit to being under too much stress, yet they feel helpless to do anything about it. They falsely assume their unhealthy level of stress is outside of their control and consequently feel trapped.

Stress can be caused by many things —financial anxiety, job pressures, family demands, over-committed schedules, deadlines, noise, poor eating habits, lack of sleep and exercise, etc. Once you have identified what is causing your stress, you are better equipped to handle it.

Most of us spend our days running at high speed, never slowing down to relax. It's easy to miss out on enjoying life, however, if we are always running around frantically trying to do things. Eliminate some activities. Slow down. Like a car set on cruise control, you need to learn to go at your own steady pace. It might appear to others as slow and unproductive, but by living this way, you are

dictating your own pace instead of letting others
rush you.

Rushing really doesn't get things done any
quicker. In fact, rushing often leads to more mistakes, which drains your energy. When you cruise
instead of rush, you still get things done, but without
the panic and stress.

Stress is an unavoidable part of life, but here are
some tips for reducing the stress in your life:

- **Focus on simply being in the moment.** Look
  around you. What beauty or enjoyment is there
  in your world right now? Let yourself fully
  experience it with the full participation of all your
  senses. Breathe it in.

  As I sit here at my computer writing, I feel the
  warmth of the sun on my arm. I observe the
  snow-covered evergreens glistening in the sun-
  light. I witness the shadows of the leaves dancing
  on the snow and hear the wind howling gently
  against the side of the house. I take note of one
  little sapling standing in the shadow of a hun-
  dred-foot-tall oak tree, trying to "measure up." I
  become aware of little children sledding down the
  hill and smile at their laughter. Simple? That's
  what it's all about — finding pleasure in small
  things.

  When you grasp what it means to be present in
  the moment — to fully experience whatever you
  are doing — the most mundane tasks and activities take on new meaning. In fact, some women
  admitted to having discovered the power of chores
  for soothing the soul. By focusing completely on
  the chore in front of you — washing dishes, fold-

ing laundry, changing sheets, vacuuming, dusting — you can turn off the frenzy of life for awhile.

Pay attention to where you are and what you are doing now rather than thinking about what has to be done and where you have to be next. Eat your meals slowly, savoring each bite. Read to your daughter or granddaughter, breathing in the smell of her hair and mentally memorizing the details of her sweet, angelic face. Sit in the warm sunshine with your spouse or neighbor and sip a cool glass of lemonade while discussing the day.

The mind can't race a hundred miles an hour and also store the color, smell, taste, touch and sound of an occasion. In order to have clear memories of all the experiences that make up a lifetime, you need to stop and smell — really smell — the proverbial rose.

- **Have fun!** Laughter helps us relax. Life isn't supposed to be all seriousness. Surprise yourself and others by your spontaneity. Steve and I once turned irrigating the grass and shrubs into an unexpected water fight. We felt like kids running around the yard chasing each other with a garden hose. I'm sure we looked ridiculous to anyone watching, but we had a blast!

Fun does not depend on an excessive outlay of cash. You don't need to plan extravagant events to have a great time. The happiest and most memorable experiences are often the unplanned, spur of the moment occasions that recharge you and strengthen your bond with others.

Carve out space in your schedule for pleasurable

activities that relax you and renew your spirit.
Resist the urge to spend Saturday cleaning your
house; instead, attend an art festival, go bike riding, pick apples, or invite friends over for a game
of cards. When you play, you are not focused on
your troubles or responsibilities, but rather,
you're fully present in the moment!

- **Strive for balance.** What good is achieving professional success if your family falls apart? What
  good will all your education and knowledge do for
  you if you lose your health? In a balanced life, your
  investment of time and energy is aligned with your
  priorities, so that you are spending the majority of
  your time doing what is important to you.

  Bringing balance to your life requires a commitment to setting personal boundaries. Set aside
  one day a week, or an hour or two throughout the
  week, for recreation. This may prove a little more
  of a challenge if you are a single working parent,
  but perhaps you can find a few hours during your
  hectic week to do something relaxing by yourself
  or with a friend.

  You might enjoy getting out in nature and walking
  by the water. We have a dam near our home, and
  I find walking over the dam to be soothing and
  tranquil, an opportunity to contemplate whatever
  is going on in my life, and the worries and concerns just seem to get washed away with the
  power of the water breaking over the dam.

  Some women enjoy the ritual of relaxing in a tub
  of hot, sudsy water to soothe their souls as well
  as their bodies. A couple years ago, Steve and I

invested in a hot tub and find our nightly soaks to be the perfect place for relaxing and reconnecting with each other after a long day. Many of the women I spoke with found gardening to be an ideal outlet for them. Luanne shared that she starts off every day with fifteen minutes "digging in the dirt" and that was enough to stimulate her mind as well as an opportunity for her to express her gratitude for another day.

Nurturing yourself also involves giving yourself an opportunity to express your creative urges. For Sue, this meant learning to play the piano. For Karen, it meant discovering herself among her brushes and paint. For Beth, it meant honoring the poetry that was inside of her. For Jolene, it was discovering her natural ability to capture breathtaking photographs and display them creatively.

- **Reach out.** Share your burdens with a close friend or family member. Don't withdraw. Let someone love you and help you see your life from a fresh perspective. My friend Anita recently did this for me when she visited me on a particularly stressful day. She literally took over. My children were home from school, so she delegated household chores. She got a delicious dinner going in the crock-pot. She screened my phone calls and helped me package some shipments that needed to go to the post office. Then she listened and helped me prioritize what else I needed to do. That's what real friends do! Let them.

I am thinking more and more of the benefits of time alone in terms of medical costs. Stress is responsible for so many of our physical problems. Doing something that takes you out of your current state of mind — especially something creative — is very beneficial. —Leslie

The best stress relief I have found is tending my flowerbeds. The physical act of pulling weeds, placing new plants in the ground, and the satisfaction of standing back and seeing a job well done really helps me. Any time I find myself facing a huge problem or a stressful situation, I start pulling weeds. Pulling a weed and throwing it away helps me release my problem, worry, or fear along with it. —Donna

Find time every day for solitude and reflective thinking

Solitude — time spent alone without distractions — is essential for our spiritual, psychological and physical health. Alone time is strictly "*you*-time" when you don't have to be doing anything for anyone else. It's a time to reconnect with yourself — without guilt! Everyone will benefit when you return from your solitude refreshed, happier, more peaceful, more focused, and ready to carry on.

If you aren't in the habit of taking time for

yourself, you may resist it, believing it's selfish to take time to nurture and pamper yourself. Ignore the voice in your head that reminds you of chores to do or paperwork to get caught up on. The truth is: *You will never be done with these things!* Your work will wait for you. You need to just let it go.

Some women have adopted the idea of having a weekly "date night" with themselves to take art classes, go to the gym, see a movie, write in a journal, visit a museum, browse in a bookstore, watch a sunset, soak in the tub by candlelight, read a novel, rent a movie, buy a magazine and read it in bed, do yoga, work on a scrapbook, tend their garden, or walk their dog. These women shared that making this time a priority in their lives served to calm their soul, support their creativity, and give them the mental space they needed to tune into their inner voice.

But where can you go to find peace and quiet? Here are a few suggestions:

- Your bedroom or another restful retreat at home.

- A local coffee shop where you can sit undisturbed with your favorite flavored latte.

- A quiet beach — nothing more soothing than the comforting swoosh of the waves against the sand.

- Your public library — built-in quiet!

- A favorite park bench where your senses are heightened by the activity of the joggers, people walking their dogs, and children playing. And, by the way...TURN OFF YOUR CELL PHONE!!

It's also important to schedule time for reflective thinking. At the end of the day, take a few moments to rewind the tape of your day and review your progress. What did you really do well? In what ways could you improve? Make reflection a daily habit.

I enjoy my time alone. I find it absolutely necessary. I need the time to refuel myself emotionally. A day without solitude makes a big difference in my overall well-being and ability to cope with life. It wasn't always this important to me, but as I get older, I find that I am getting more enjoyment out of being alone. My own company is more than sufficient. —Cynthia

I love my own company! I am perfectly capable of entertaining myself for hours on end. Of course I love the company of others too, but I need that "me-time" with no one else around to do what I want and totally recharge. —Ginny

Commit to daily exercise as a way of life

The benefits of daily exercise combined with a nutritious diet, plenty of water, and adequate sleep are numerous. Staying in top physical condition during transition not only increases physical health, but it also gives you a psychological boost. Fitness expert Kathy Smith turned to exercise after the loss of both her parents at a young age. She discovered running and strength training did more to help alleviate her depression and grief than anything else she tried.

Nearly all the women I interviewed relied on some type of physical exercise as a foundation for living a healthier and more productive life. When you make a habit of exercising first thing in the morning, it energizes you for the whole day. Your physical activity can be running on a treadmill, swimming laps, inline skating, biking, kayaking, karate, or simply taking a walk outside near your home.

No matter what you do for a workout, you will discover that the act of exercising communicates to your mind that you are a healthy person. If you focus primarily on weight loss, you're telling your mind that in reality you are overweight and so your body supports those thoughts. If you focus on creating a healthy lifestyle, however, you'll be much more motivated and your body will support your thoughts that you're a healthy person. Pilates first thing in the morning suddenly becomes a time of soulful renewal as well as a way to keep your body strong and flexible.

I have become more self-aware. My personal habits have changed, including working out with weights, walking and jogging for exercise. I relish the sensation of my own body. I value relationships and work at maintaining them. For me that has meant sharing with other women some of our feelings of success and failure. I try to bring balance to my work and personal life by being conscious of my decisions about how much time to devote to each. I have given up watching television. I am more disciplined about personal goals. —Maryanne

*The "me" stage is when we reconnect with ourselves. We will pass through this phase and then let our knowledge about our true self dictate our actions for the rest of our lives. My reconnection started when I woke up from the deep sleep of just drifting through life, doing what was expected of me. Now I want to and **need** to listen to my authentic self, and I finally have the drive to act on whatever I hear. For instance, I heard a voice saying that health was critical and started walking and lifting weights. I wanted to be an active participant in life so I examined my habits and started afresh. —Sabrina*

I see so many women my age not looking well. Many of my friends are battling cancer. One woman I know ate poorly and drank soft drinks all her life and now her body is just shutting down. I really believe good nutrition is so important. I try to eat healthy. I buy organic foods and read labels. I avoid hydrogenated oil, boxed foods, alcohol (although I like wine occasionally), and cigarettes. I eat lots of soy products, cherry juice, green tea, protein shakes, and raw oatmeal on all natural cereal with honey and soymilk, raw vegetables, lots of salads, and organic meat. Does all this really help? Well, I certainly don't feel like I'm 53! —Joyce

Create a sanctuary at home

Women need to have a space of their own, a sanctuary apart from the rest of their lives where they can go to renew their spirit. Men do this all the time — a favorite chair, woodshop, or garage. You deserve this, too! We all need a spot where we can escape to collect our thoughts, but how do you create your personal oasis for peaceful, uninterrupted time alone?

Your bedroom is the most logical choice for a quiet escape, but it's also a room that many women share with someone else. So define an area — perhaps a reading chair in a sunny corner by the window — and make it your own. Cozy up your space with plush pillows, a soft chenille throw, and a fluffy rug underfoot. Select calming music, light a scented candle, and open the window to let in a gentle breeze. Include a pretty potted plant, some fragrant hand lotion, a treasured photograph, and maybe a few cherished keepsakes. Fill a basket with attractive stationery for an impromptu note to a friend, books and magazines you want to read, and your journal for jotting down sudden thoughts or insights that come to your mind during your quiet, reflective time.

On the other hand, your private sanctuary might be an art or craft table. Perhaps scrapbooking, rubber-stamping, or sewing provides you with the break you need from the rest of the world in order to renew your spirit. Martha set up her artist's easel in a corner of her basement that gets lots of natural light.

"I think it's so important to have time to yourself — especially when you're married," says Martha.

"You need a place to get away from everybody when you feel the need. I retreat to my easel where I can go to be alone and paint. I keep the window open just a bit so I can hear the birds chirping. It's absolutely the best part of my day!"

Where's your dream spot? When the weather's nice, you could retreat to a sun porch, patio, or secluded garden spot. Hang up a hammock or lounge in an Adirondack chair.

To create an environment that nurtures your soul, you will need to identify and eliminate what's draining you. When my environment is cluttered and disorganized, I feel cluttered and disorganized. I know you've heard it before, but the first step to a restful retreat at home is removing the clutter!

When you are surrounded by open, organized space, you feel more creative and in control. Clearing out the physical clutter in your life helps you clear out the mental clutter as well. By disposing of unneeded items that no longer serve you, you're making space for the new things that will renew your spirit. For instance, when I lost fifty pounds last year, I ruthlessly went through my closet and dresser drawers to get rid of anything that no longer fit or didn't make me feel great wearing it. I was left with a pretty bare closet! But slowly, I began to find pieces that I truly loved wearing and reflected who I am now.

Scarcity is a mind-set that says you must hold onto what you have for fear that you may not get something better. My mother's generation, who lived during the Depression era, had this philosophy so well ingrained into them that even today they will hoard things for "someday." Ann Wells writes of going through her sister's belongings after her untimely death and is reminded of how futile it is to hang onto expensive clothing, china dishes, crystal, luxurious linens and perfume that you never use. "Don't ever save anything for a special occasion," says Wells. "Every day you're alive is a special occasion."

You don't need to do this all in one weekend! Daily progress is what's important. Set aside a certain amount of time every day (even if it's only fifteen minutes) to tackle one small area. Be ruthless. Throw away what you must, sell what you can, and give the rest to charity.

I've always needed my alone time...to read, to paint, and to just doze to some smooth jazz. —Lilly

Our family recently downsized to a smaller home and we all love it! So often our society tells us that bigger and more expensive are better, but we have felt such freedom in getting rid of a lot of stuff from our lives. We now feel as if we have more time. Also, we have less money tied up in a house, so we're free to use that money for our family. To anyone considering this kind of change: Go for it! You'll be glad you did. —Patti Leppo, Marietta, GA (excerpted from a letter to BH&G/April 2003)

Make each day count!

Do something you love every single day. Annie Dillard, author of *Pilgrim at Tinker Creek,* said, "How we spend our days is, of course, how we spend our lives." The question to you then is, how are you spending your days? Ask yourself, "Is the way I'm spending my time reflecting my true priorities? Is this activity contributing to my bigger goals?"

Schedule time every day to do something that makes you happy. Stop putting it off! Is there a way to incorporate the activities that nurture and renew your spirit into your life now? If we waited until the time was absolutely right, many of us would never get to do what we really want to do. Perhaps you are putting off your enjoyment until you have more time, or more money, or some other improved condition. The trouble with that is that it might never happen, or it may be too long in coming.

I've always enjoyed movies and novels that have parallel plots where the story could play out one of two ways depending on a decision or choice that the main character makes early in the action. You are at a turning point in your life. The decisions you make right now will affect what happens at the end of your story. If you're not happy with the direction your life is going, you can start right here, right now to create a new ending. Decide today to make the changes necessary so that you are spending the majority of your time doing what is important to you.

We all need to focus more on ourselves as we grow older. It isn't a selfish thing; it's necessary for our survival. —Linda

The "me" stage is wonderful! I still am in it and I feel so good pursuing different goals, discovering new aspects about myself, and just getting to know the current me. I am having a blast rediscovering myself! —Gina

Action Steps:

1. Write down all of the things that are causing stress in your life, including any recent changes. Decide whether or not you have any control over the circumstances that are causing your stress. Deal with the things that you can control and stop worrying about the things that you cannot.

2. Make a list of your favorite ways to recharge. They can be as simple as soaking in the bathtub, taking a walk before dinner, or lighting candles and listening to calming music while curling up with a good book. You might want to pick up some Chinese take-out and rent a DVD for a relaxing evening at home. Once in awhile, consider indulging in a therapeutic massage or slipping away to a bed-and-breakfast for a quiet weekend by yourself.

3. Block out one evening a week for the next six months just for you. See a movie, visit a museum, or take a class — whatever it takes for you to feel personally rejuvenated.

4. Create a personal retreat at home — a place that is all yours where you can go to collect your thoughts and renew your spirit.

5. Try out different types of physical activity. You might discover that you like kickboxing, fencing, or golf. Don't be afraid to experiment. Start today incorporating physical activity into your daily schedule.

CHAPTER FIVE: SHORE UP YOUR RELATIONSHIPS

"Friendship improves happiness and
abates misery by the doubling of our joy
and the dividing of our grief."

— *Cicero*

Surround yourself with good friends

As you mature, you'll discover that personal relationships become increasingly important in your life. A positive connection with your family — the most important group of people you will ever belong to — is vital to your sense of belonging. And a key relationship with a close friend can be the "solid ground" you need during turbulent times.

At midlife, your friendships with other women will make the difference between living a vibrant, fulfilling life and being miserably alone. Every woman longs for someone who will listen and offer a safe environment where she can express her feelings. Several women I spoke with reported that a small group of friends they meet with weekly or bi-weekly for coffee were the source of strength that sustained them during a time of change. Friends cheer you on while you explore your different options, catch you when you fall, and encourage and support you as you endeavor to redefine yourself.

Even when life gets busy, make time with your friends a priority. Spend time with them, do fun things together, and experience how much more enjoyable life is when you share it with those closest to you.

If you haven't already, take time to cultivate meaningful relationships. Find interesting, fun people! If you want to meet people with similar interests, join a club or association, take a class, or volunteer for a cause or project that you believe in. Being involved in an ongoing activity and meeting with the same people on a regular basis gives you an opportunity to get to know them before you decide to pursue a more personal relationship.

When Sue joined the Sierra Club, she not only discovered a new activity she really enjoys, but she met many new friends as well — including her partner. Sue also attends a weekly business-networking group where in addition to picking up new leads for her design business, she's cultivated relationships with people who share her energy for life.

You may experience a natural affiliation with women who, like you, are grappling with the unique challenges and adjustments that occur at midlife. These are women with whom you can share the joys and struggles of the journey. Talk to them. Share your stories. Sometimes talking to others keeps you from thinking you're going crazy!

That's one reason that the Red Hat Society has become so popular in recent years. Inspired by the poem "Warning" by Jenny Joseph, Sue Ellen Cooper gave her friend a bright red fedora for her birthday. Soon other friends began to expect the unique gift for fiftieth birthdays and beyond. Since the narrator of the poem dares when she is old to "...wear purple and a red hat which doesn't go, and doesn't suit me..." the women bought matching purple outfits and began meeting for tea and other fun outings. The idea caught on and now new groups are popping up all over the country.

I try not to over-schedule myself, which is difficult because I'm very work-oriented. But I've learned not to let myself get overloaded so I have time to take care of myself through yoga, bike-riding, and daily meditation. I find that connecting with nature, homeotherapy sessions if I'm feeling toxic, and being with my family really helps to center me and conserves my physical and mental energy. Spending an afternoon with my son, talking with my parents or siblings, or preparing a beautiful meal with Jack, really helps me to stay balanced and I feel more grounded. —Tricia

Take off the masks

One of life's great rewards is developing intimate relationships with other people, yet the only way to enter that level of closeness is through open honesty and transparency. Take off the masks! Stop pretending! Friends see your imperfections, but they also recognize your strengths. Friends offer you the opportunity to be yourself.

It can be scary to lower your defenses and open up your life to others because you risk rejection. It's tempting to put up emotional barriers and try to disconnect from the world around you in an attempt to avoid getting hurt. However, when you reveal your feelings of frustration and fear of failure to your closest friends and they stand by you, you experience a sense of acceptance and understanding. Vulnerability is the key to intimacy.

I forgive myself for not understanding the importance of relationships. I forgive myself for my lack of communication with my parents after I left the nest. I forgive myself for avoiding relationships, for the long deep sleep during my marriage, and for the isolation that came masquerading as independence. I forgive the part of me that hid from relationships as a way to avoid pain and hurt. I forgive the years of denying my feelings, avoiding getting to know my true self. —Sam

Most of us aren't as mature and immune to being hurt as we would like the world to think. I feel that learning and being able to admit those truths bring us closer to people as they see the real us, not some front we put onto the world. —Nancy

Avoid negativity!

You become like the people you hang out with so ask yourself, "Who do I spend time with? Where do they have me going? What do they have me thinking about? What do they have me becoming? If you want to be successful, you must hang out with successful people.

Mark Victor Hansen tells the story of wanting to move from millionaire status to billionaire status. He asked Tony Robbins what he was doing wrong. Tony asked, "Who are you hanging out with?" Mark responded that all of his friends were millionaires. "Well, that's your problem," replied Tony. "If you want to be a billionaire, you have to hang around with billionaires."

Most likely you're not concerned with moving from millionaire status to billionaire status but, nonetheless, envisioning a better life for yourself can be threatening to those around you. It's human nature for people to reject what they don't understand and have no personal experience with. People fear the unknown and unknowingly dismiss new ideas because anything new or strange makes them feel uncomfortable.

If you have friends, relatives, or coworkers who you believe are unsupportive, or possibly a detriment to your success, block them out — *now!* Intentionally surround yourself with optimistic, upbeat people. After your friends and family begin to see your dream materialize, they will likely show their support. Meanwhile, keep listening to positive, encouraging words from women who have already achieved success with goals and dreams similar to yours.

Like a patchwork quilt, I'm a little bit of everybody I've met. I've tried over the years to incorporate the good things of others into my own life. I'm inspired by other people's energy. Sometimes, however, it becomes necessary to delete relationships that may have run their course. They may have been wonderful at one time, but they no longer hold any value. I don't waste my time with people that don't in some way feed me or energize me. Chronic negativity zaps my energy. If someone is just going through a difficult time, that's one thing, but when you realize that someone's never going to change and they continually feed off of you, you're not doing either one of you a favor by hanging on. —Libby

I maintain my positive attitude by reading inspiring stories, listening to tapes and CDs in my car, and staying connected to people. I stay in shape by running regularly. I started running over twenty years ago when I quit smoking and it's been one of the smartest choices I've ever made. Next month, I'm running in a marathon with my daughter in Arizona. It'll be fun to do it together! It requires a time commitment and discipline to train for it, of course, but I've gotten so much out of it. It's just one way that I take time for myself. I also pray, meditate, and journal daily. It helps keep me grounded. —Tess

Establish a mastermind group

An exceptionally effective way to speed up your success in any new endeavor is to ask others how to tackle the challenges that you face. A mastermind group is an ideal way to accomplish this on a regular basis. Preferably, your group should consist of four to six ambitious, goal-oriented women who are likely to create synergy and who want to develop a long-term relationship. The group provides a unique forum for sharing ideas and information. These are women who will support you in your growth, challenge you to be your best, and encourage you when your vision becomes clouded.

Surround yourself with those who will remind you that you're capable and encourage you to "go for it." I'm reminded of the movie *Calendar Girls* in which a handful of ladies from Yorkshire got together and decided to raise money for a new sofa in the relatives' waiting room at the local hospital. To date, they have raised over one million US dollars and built an entire new leukemia wing for the hospital in addition to the sofa! These middle-aged gals prove that with the support of like-minded women, you can achieve almost anything.

Find a coach

A coach is person who motivates you to clarify your aspirations and achieve your goals. Unlike a therapist who helps "fix" a client's problems, a coach's job is to encourage your personal and professional development in a secure and supportive environment. While a therapist assists a client in examining the past, a coach's focus is on helping you speed up your progress so you can accomplish your objectives.

Working with a coach can be an excellent investment — especially during a time of transition. In fact, I contracted with a coach to get me through the final stages of completing this book because I was blocked and needed direction. But working with a professional coach is not always financially feasible. If this is your case, you can work with a friend.

Select somebody with similar drive and ambition to yours — a woman who is seeking greater authenticity in her own life and who is pursuing her dreams. While it's not necessary for this person to have the same goal, a commitment to the process is crucial. You don't even need to live in close proximity to this person because it's so easy these days to communicate via email or telephone. In fact, many professional coaches only accept telephone clients.

Arrange for a brainstorming session in which you establish goals for what you hope to accomplish. Agree on a target date for achieving your objectives (three to six months is ideal) and then reevaluate how you've done and where you want to go from there.

If you elect to have a friend coach you, it is vitally important that you specify certain times for weekly review of your progress. Before each session, be clear about what you hope to accomplish. Expect her to hold you accountable to your commitment. Someone who is not emotionally involved in your situation can frequently determine what's blocking you and ask compelling, thought-provoking questions that will guide you to discovering your own solutions.

My sisters are my best friends; I would rather have five loyal, dedicated friends than one hundred casual acquaintances. I'm very open and honest with people and expect that kind of transparency in return. If I give too much without receiving, it wears on me. I don't tolerate negative people in my life either. I'm not talking about the people who are down or have the "blues," but people who just can't ever find the good in anything. —Maureen

It really is true! Losing someone does give you a better set of priorities. It shifts the emphasis to the dearness of those I am close to. I don't take them for granted as much as I used to do. Life is sacred and the death of a parent, or close friend, is a reminder of how sacred it is. —Meg

Action Steps:

1. Write down the names of family and friends, mentors, spiritual advisors, and anyone who is special in your life outside the business world. Review the amount of time you spend with these people. Are "peripheral" relationships robbing you of time that would be better spent developing your core relationships? Protect your family and personal time!

2. Talk to a few friends you respect and trust — women who are pursuing their dream — and form a mastermind group. Set up a regular meeting schedule and a format you will follow for your meetings so you stay on track.

3. If you don't have the kind of friends you want in your life, then join an association, take a class, or volunteer for a project that interests you. You'll have more opportunities to get to know some new people with similar interests.

4. Find a coach. [There are several websites on the Internet where you can find someone who is right for you.] Or, you can approach a friend about establishing a coaching relationship. This needs to be someone you trust as well as someone who knows you well enough to ask the tough questions.

5. Form a Path Partners group. I mentioned this previously in Chapter One. A Path Partners group is a great way to meet with other women who are on a similar path. Course materials and guidelines for setting up your own groups are available at www.PathPartners.com.

CHAPTER SIX:
RENEW YOUR "WOWS!"

"Love does not consist in gazing at each
other, but in looking outward together
in the same direction."
—Antoine de Saint-Exupéry

Last December, Steve and I decided to renew our marriage vows while on vacation in Mexico with three other couples. We wanted our closest, most intimate friends to experience this time of renewal with us. It didn't hurt that one of the individuals "just happened" to be our pastor!

We planned the ceremony for the evening of our third day in Cancun. Steve ordered flowers and a cake to be delivered to the suite in advance of the scheduled ceremony. Wanting to confirm that everything had been delivered according to plan, our concierge called the suite and said in his thick, Mexican accent, "I understand that you're renewing your *wows!*" Brian, our pastor, was the one who took the call and couldn't resist using the twist on words during the lovely ceremony he performed for us. We indeed were renewing our "WOWS!"

Marriage, when it is going well, makes you feel like a million bucks, but when there's conflict, tension, and unresolved issues, it negatively impacts every area of your life.

My biggest accomplishment has been staying married for 27 years. When I was younger, I was hotheaded and always needed to be right; now that I'm older, I'm mellower and don't need to be right all the time. —Joyce

So many marriages fall apart in midlife. Couples just look at each other and say, 'I don't even know you!' You really have to work at a marriage if you want a long-lasting, gratifying relationship. —Inge

Change yourself first

Don't rely on your husband to meet all of your needs. A mate enlarges and enriches your life and contributes to your happiness, but if you rely too heavily on a partner for fulfillment, you'll cripple the relationship. Authentic, mature love is based on appreciation, affection, and mutual respect. When you do those things, your relationship with your husband becomes less dependent and more *inter*-dependent.

About three years ago, Arlene's husband confessed that he had cheated on her. He said it was just one incident, but it didn't matter to her if it was one time or one hundred times. She lost her trust in him and ended up temporarily leaving him.

"That's when my midlife crisis began," Arlene said. "What next? Do I throw it all away or find out why it happened and try to resolve it?"

Arlene secretly thought that ending the marriage would be the easy thing to do, but she made the difficult decision to stick with it.

"It took several months before I could even look at him and tell him what I was feeling. I don't think he realized how badly he'd hurt me. I think men generally think of sex as something separate than love and that 'it was only once' isn't so bad because after all, it was *only* sex."

During the marriage therapy that followed, Arlene realized that the two of them had been standing still in their marriage for a long time. It's so easy to wake up, go to work, come home, and fill your time with laundry, kids, and chores, and completely forget about the two of you as a married couple.

"I realized that although we had both set personal and career goals, we'd neglected to set any marriage goals. So now we have weekly 'check-in' sessions where we can talk honestly about anything. We both realize that we really are better as a team and that our lives do belong together. I still struggle with self-esteem issues and I have fleeting thoughts about what happened, but John and I are strong now and we're going to be okay.

"Funny how you think the one thing that will kill you actually makes you view life in a different light. Until John's confession, I only saw myself as John's wife. After being forced to deal with who I am as an individual, I see how my life could have been and thank God for knowing what it would take to change direction."

At midlife, you can no longer afford to pretend that anyone other than yourself is going to bring you the fulfillment you long for. Women at midlife are no longer looking for a man to give their lives meaning or to define them. You can no longer rely on anyone, not even a devoted partner, for what you most deeply want and need. It's time to assume responsibility for your own life — your individual growth and personal happiness.

Midlife women want a partner with whom they can be vulnerable and share their fears and insecurities. They desire a companion, friend and playmate — someone to share interests and activities with. Midlife women want someone who will share and support their dreams.

How often have you heard women say, "My marriage would be great if only my husband would change?" It's not uncommon for couples that have been married for many years to feel that their connection has grown stagnant. The challenge is how to make significant changes in your marriage without sacrificing the best of what you have.

Choose to forgive your husband when he has disappointed you. And be willing to confess when you've been wrong. The key to a sincere apology is to say, "I'm sorry" without adding, "but..." Asking what you can do to repair the damage demonstrates your desire to take responsibility for your own mistakes and work together to create a loving, supportive relationship.

Stop making those nasty remarks! It's so easy to

be critical, but it's also detrimental. Let go of the little irritations that naturally come with living with another person. Instead, appreciate your husband's attempts to change annoying habits and make a conscious effort to focus on his positive character traits. Look for occasions to praise him and express gratitude for all he does — positive reinforcement can go a long way!

Commit to making the rest of your marriage the best yet.

Keep the lines of communication open

Once a week, perhaps on Sunday evening, sit down with each other and discuss any current issues: decisions that need to be made, creative solutions for problems that you may be facing, ways to make one another feel more loved and appreciated, and areas in which you or your spouse may require additional support.

If one or both of you are going through a transition period — whether due to an empty nest, career change, life-threatening illness, adjustment to a new body image after a significant weight loss, or entering retirement —exploring changes with your spouse can revitalize your relationship and strengthen your bond. By all means, if you need counseling, then schedule an appointment. But don't let the demands of life keep you from the opportunity to create a deeper intimacy through a trusting, abiding friendship with your spouse.

In midlife, relationships become much more important. It's critical that both partners have their needs met. Do you have quiet time for the two of you? Do you talk candidly about your relationship and your sexual needs? Are you able to set aside time to go out once a week and just have fun?

Men tend to not openly discuss midlife issues as much as women for the same reasons that prevent them from asking for directions; they like to think they can find their own way without consulting a road map. I'd like to think this is changing, however, and that men are learning the value of asking some of the tough questions that allow them to maneuver successfully through their middle years. Encourage your husband to talk to you. Remember to be supportive and non-judgmental. He is also going through a transition.

Midlife is a time when you can finally acknowledge what you need to make yourself happy. The problem is that so much of a woman's value in our culture comes from her ability to anticipate and meet the needs of others. When she becomes more vocal about her needs, it often creates conflict in her marriage relationship. This makes it difficult to express your needs without feeling guilty and selfish. But when you don't feel heard, or don't dare to voice your needs, you tend to shut down. You may continue to function for a while, but you'll eventually become isolated and even withdrawn. When you hold back on intimacy, you hold back on life.

Work as a team to get through the difficult times rather than fighting with each other. You got married to become one — to be partners together — not competitors against one another. When you stop pointing fingers and start talking about your own needs, it will open the doors to honest, non-accusing communication. A good marriage relationship will nurture you and create energy that carries over into every aspect of your life.

Life has been really difficult. I am in the midst of menopause. I tried estrogen, but the prog-esterone that came with it nearly made me psychotic, so I am going it alone now with just Evista for my bones. My husband, however, ran out of patience and we've started divorce proceedings. It's doubly hard to go through this alone. He has abandoned our grown chil-dren and me completely. I suspect he is in the middle of a midlife crisis of his own. —Ellen

I'm intelligent. I want to do something with my life, but anything I want to do comes after the kids and my husband. I have to put everyone else first and then even when I do what I want to do, I feel guilty. It's very frustrating. I'm tired of trying to make everyone happy and take care of everyone else's needs. We chose to have our kids later in life, but now I feel like I'm hauling them through life. My husband travels several days every week and when he comes home wanting attention, I'm completely exhausted. There's just nothing left of me. He tries to help, but he doesn't know our routines so he just ends up being in the way. He's more like a frequent visitor. —Marijo

Rediscover the joy of being together

Many midlife women wonder, "Why doesn't it feel the same as it did before?" It isn't that you no longer love one another; it's just that you have become set in a routine — like going around a racetrack in endless circles, doing the same things every day. You begin to take each other for granted. Many couples get their priorities out of order without even realizing it. Unfortunately, when these feelings come on, there's a tendency to think that means the end of a marriage. Your marriage isn't over; it's just fallen asleep and you need to wake it up!

Fun plays a huge part in what makes people fall in love in the first place. Couples who nurture the fun part of their relationship create a wonderful emotional climate for their marriage.

Having fun together involves spending time together that's enjoyable for both of you, but it doesn't have to be elaborate or expensive. Check out places that the two of you have never been before. Different surroundings are a wonderful way to rekindle some of the passion the two of you used to share.

You can rent a canoe for a lazy trip down the river or dust off your bikes for an excursion to your local ice cream parlor. Go to a park and swing on the swings or play a round of miniature golf. Check your paper for outdoor concerts in your area. Karen and her husband frequently enjoy packing a picnic supper and taking in a jazz concert at the park. "We just spread out a blanket and enjoy the music."

Visit a nearby coffee shop with big, overstuffed sofas to curl up with a latté and talk. Or perhaps a long walk through the woods holding hands may be all you need to get away from the demands at home or the office and enjoy time alone together.

Determine to relax and have fun with your mate, but don't be too disappointed if the magic doesn't come back on the first date. Improving your marriage is a process. Be persistent and be patient. Anything worthwhile is worth your time and effort.

If you still have younger children at home, you may feel that you're neglecting them by leaving them with a sitter for a couple hours while the two of you work on your relationship. This couldn't be farther from the truth! Children gain a deep sense of security when they see that their parents are passionately in love with each other. By putting your husband first and not letting your life revolve around your kids, you're setting a wonderful example for your children and everyone benefits.

Never use date night to discuss volatile issues! Vow not to bring up topics such as the MasterCard bill when you're out. If you and your husband have totally different interests — one of you likes backpacking and the other one prefers the theatre — try some of the activities your husband enjoys and vice versa. And maybe try finding other like-minded, fun-loving couples to hang out with.

Sanyika's idea of a relaxing vacation was a trip to the beach or visiting a spa, but when her husband had the opportunity to plan their next getaway, he took them "jeep jammin" — the furthest thing from Sanyika's mind. But she went along anyway and discovered she loved it! Now they have a new hobby they can enjoy together.

A deeply committed relationship with your husband can provide you with a lifelong companion to share fun and exhilarating times with, a satisfying sexual connection, and the wonderful feeling that someone is on your side.

Rekindle your sexual relationship. You've probably heard a friend say, "My marriage has lost its spark and I have no idea why." You can't expect the same level of success in your marriage relationship as you do in other areas of your life without putting forth the same kind of effort. If you're too tired at night to set aside even a little time for your husband or you're too busy nagging and complaining about what he didn't do instead of recognizing the small gestures he makes to show his love, then you're playing as much a part in the stagnation of your marriage as your husband is.

It's so easy to get stuck in a rut and forget how great sex can be! Perhaps your relationship has become monotonous or routine. Several tastefully written guides are on the market today for couples desiring to add spark to their love life. You might arrange to meet your husband at home during the day for a romantic rendezvous. Candles and soft music can go a long way towards setting the mood.

Maybe you have unrealistic expectations for how you should look. If you don't feel good about your body, you'll feel unattractive and vulnerable. It's all in your attitude. Imagine how you would act if you were totally uninhibited. Get comfortable with your body. Accept yourself the way you are. If you need to firm up, then take the necessary steps to get into shape. But don't rob yourself of the joy and satisfaction that comes from a loving connection with your spouse.

Sex is a wonderful way to connect emotionally and spiritually with your husband, but you can only make that connection when you make yourself available. If your hectic schedule leaves you feeling exhausted at the end of the day, you need to make your relationship a priority and give it the attention it deserves. You and your husband can enjoy a vibrant sex life now and for many years to come. Remember that the success of your marriage is a choice, not some random act of luck or fate.

You know what I like about being older? I like that I'm comfortable with my body and I know how to make love. At forty, I have more of a sex drive than I did at twenty-five or thirty. Stamina not withstanding, I think older men and women make better lovers because we understand that sex is more than just a physical event. —Gwen

I got to a point where I wanted to change every-thing — my clothes, my house, my life! I was tired of wearing jeans and old sweatshirts all the time. I wanted to look more sophisticated, more grown up more sexy! —Melinda

Avoid temptation

The poet John Milton said, "He who reigns within himself and rules his passions, desires and fears is more than a king." Are you worried you'll lose your ability to stir lust in the opposite sex? Why would you even want to try to allure someone else — so you can soothe your frail, aging ego by proving to yourself that you're still sexy?

Michelle went through most of her life doing things that other people do — always looking for something, but not knowing what it was. She got married thinking that was the best thing for her and that having two children was the answer. Time proved her wrong.

"It just opened my eyes to the fact that I wasn't cut out to be a mother, but because I loved my children I did the best I could," she said. "I stayed married and suffered through the hormonal ups and downs of having children and a not-so-good marriage. I put my children first and my husband second. I came in somewhere between the dog and the cat."

Michelle thought things were okay until her late thirties when she experienced a "crush" that knocked her socks off.

"It really threw me for a loop. The chemistry was so strong it scared me. I was totally unprepared for anything like that. I was very surprised at how powerful a reaction I had to someone for no apparent reason. I never considered that possibility when I got married. I just assumed it would be my husband forever and no one else."

The attraction brought a lot of buried issues to the surface and marked the beginning of a wild ride through a serious midlife crisis.

"So there I am, in-lust with one person and married to someone else. It opened my eyes to myself in a lot of ways. I began to question my love for my husband. I just knew it couldn't compete with my 'new love.'"

Michelle looked for an escape, but found none when she considered her lack of education, poor employment record, and her two children. She even considered a low-wage, part-time job such as working at McDonald's.

"I wondered, where would I go? My parents' home? I doubt it. I got married to escape that so why should I go back there? It just didn't make sense to me that I should live almost thirty-eight years to end up at McDonald's. It made me despondent. I felt like I deserved more than that. It's like, 'I came this far for *that?*' I stayed feeling like that for a long time. They were honestly the worst years of my life," she admits.

Things got pretty rough for Michelle and her husband as a couple until they realized there was some work they both had to do, changes they needed to make. Eventually they began the slow, agonizing process of actually building a relationship.

"Since experiencing my crush, I look at men differently. I value my husband because he has so many characteristics that I find attractive — deep concern for his family and he provides such stability for both of us," Michelle said. "It really drilled home how powerful attraction can be, and I can understand now how many marriages get side-swiped by it."

Temptation is everywhere and adultery is advertised as something sweet to eat, but it doesn't warn you of the heartbreak afterwards. You need to give your thoughts to your husband throughout the day. You need to devote the rest of your life to trying to make his life better, more enjoyable. If he's not doing the same, you need to accept him where he is right now. Communicate your needs to him even if it causes conflict. Your relationship can't grow without occasional discomfort.

> *When I met my husband and the "fireworks" went off, I thought it had to be love! The sex was great, but I didn't have a clue what to do when it began to cool down. So I just fell into my role of "mother of us all" — including my husband. So many women get married and have children before they know anything about themselves and I was no exception. I was looking for love like everyone else and thought it was this grand explosion. Being so naïve, I confused lust with love.*
>
> *I was dreadfully unhappy. It was me though; I needed to be happy with myself, but I didn't know what I needed to be happy. I have come to realize that you can be happy under most conditions if you are happy with yourself. I no longer need, or expect, my husband to make me happy. I feel really good about myself. If you are happy with yourself and who you are as a person, it's easier to face the problems that come your way. —Naomi*

I'm turning fifty in March and I'd be lying if I didn't say aging sucks. You get to the point where men don't look at you like they used to, but that's probably better anyway. Your body chemistry can do some crazy things sometimes and if you don't run from temptation, you'll live to regret it. I've had therapy clients who went through an affair and they've all said that it's just not worth it. Roger and I always go out together on the weekends. To keep a marriage going for over thirty years, you really have to put some effort into it. Five years ago, I started learning to play golf just so we could spend more time together. I try to be into what he is into — it really helps to keep our marriage vital and healthy. —Tess

Grow together by dreaming together

Karen waited until she was older to get married and has subsequently stood by her husband during his life-threatening illness. They dream someday of living part of the year on a tropical island retreat where he can give sailing lessons and she can paint.

Get together as a couple and determine where you want to live. What kind of a house do you want? What kind of hobbies or interests do you want to pursue? Is there a business you'd like to start together? Talk about what you'll do when your children leave home or when you've saved enough for your dream vacation. Plan that trip to Italy that you've always wanted to take. Read travel books together. Study the language, the art, and the cuisine. Learn about the geography of the country and map out where you will visit.

Make dream building a part of your daily life. One couple drew closer by planning their dream cottage together. Magic starts to happen when husband and wife dream together. How can your relationship get stale when you're excited about the future? How can you *grow* apart when you are *planning* together? How can you fall out of love when you love sharing ideas and life with each other?

This long-term vision is crucial to a committed relationship because it says, "I'll be here for you and you'll be here for me." Dreaming together, thinking of life's possibilities and working in tandem toward your common goals will keep your marriage fresh and exciting. Rely on each other for support and never let yourself or your spouse lose hope. Life is a wonderful journey and together you are unstoppable!

I lost all feelings for my husband for about five years or so, maybe even a little longer. It took all my strength just to come home at night. I am not proud of many of the things I have done in my life. I can look back, however, and see the whys behind the actions and what I have learned about myself from them.

I think most things happen for a reason and something as difficult as having an affair happens for a reason too. A lot of times it is to open our eyes to ourselves. What is missing that leads us to this action? For one thing, it comes from a sense of not really knowing ourselves. If we don't know ourselves, how can we know each other?

Those feelings have since returned. I grew a lot as a person during those years. Maybe I had to let go of him emotionally to grow, even though we lived together under the same roof. Maybe it was necessary to stop focusing on him and let go of those feelings to give myself the space and strength, which I really needed at that time to make some changes to redirect my life. So maybe when people lose those feelings for each other, it's not necessarily time for a divorce, but just time for yourself. —Carly

All of a sudden, I felt that I was getting older. For me, it was as though I woke up one day with the thought, "Hey, life is passing me by and I don't want to miss it."

Was I still desirable to another man, I wondered? I started fantasizing about the men I met and their availability. I started flirting with men. I thought about going to bars alone, all the while listening to songs of infidelity. I searched "affairs" on the web and read the personals. I was craving the fun, the excitement and adventure of an affair and the passionate sex that I was sure I was missing out on.

I was in the "me" stage of midlife. It absorbed me; it was an obsession. I was looking out for only my own pleasures. After fifteen years of raising a family, I wanted fun for me. *Sex at home was quick and quiet so the girls wouldn't hear. Then we'd fall asleep to awake to another day of work. In my mind, I deserved an affair. It was what I believed I needed to feel alive again, to feel passionate about life once more.*

Then, unexpectedly, my inner voice demanded me to listen to her. "Didn't you read the article where the husband poured his heart out in grief because his wife had an affair? Didn't you read of the difficulty of forgiving a spouse and rebuilding a trusting relationship? Don't you remember the emotional breakdowns of the children? And for what — a nervous, guilt-ridden lustful act with a stranger?" My inner voice demanded that I think of those I love and the lives I would impact.

It's tempting and exciting when a nice, sweet man pays attention to you, makes you laugh and feel special. But my inner voice reprimanded me, "Work on the marriage. If it's not salvageable, then end it officially. Don't confuse the issue with the added complications that an affair poses."

I think midlife forces us to reexamine ourselves and confront our doubts. If we acted on every selfish thought and desire without thinking about the final outcome, without foreseeing or caring what could occur, who we could hurt (including ourselves), then we are basically just an unloving, selfish person. Some people refuse to listen to their inner voice that tells them right from wrong. If a marriage is on the rocks, why not talk about it and put the energy you'd use chasing that exciting fling and invest it in something real. —Linda

I stopped loving him for a long time. I also told him that and said that I was leaving as soon as I was in a position financially. There were many days that all that kept me from walking out the door were my three boys. During all this, my husband remained as in love with me as ever. He bent over backwards to keep our marriage together when all I wanted to do was leave. I think it was my unhappiness with life in general that made me want to leave. I was blaming him for my own unhappiness.

Midlife can be taxing on a marriage. Mine survived only because of my husband. I had wanted to throw it all away. I was so unhappy; I just wanted to leave everything behind. Finding out who I am helped me enormously and consequently my marriage. I think that's a big roadblock for many couples. So many go into marriage thinking the other person will make them happy and when they don't, they blame their spouse instead of taking responsibility for their own happiness.

As our love has grown and matured for each other, as we have learned to accept each other and not try to change each other, as we have allowed each other a bit of personal space, the chemistry has also deepened. Where once it was like a bonfire, it now glows smooth and steady like the coals. Our relationship is better in every respect today than it was in the beginning. No, I don't look at him and the fireworks go off, but (smile) it doesn't take much more than that! —Laurie

Action Steps:

1. Go to the bookstore and buy a relationship book that looks interesting. Read from it twenty minutes a day and apply what you have learned.

2. Write your wedding vows down somewhere where you can see them daily. Everyday renew your commitment to your marriage.

3. Plan three date night activities and schedule them on your calendar. These don't have to be evening activities; you can meet for lunch and go to an art museum.

4. Make a point of thanking your husband every day for a week for whatever he has contributed to the relationship that day.

5. Keep a memory album of your relationship. Include photos of important events, notes and cards you have sent one another, and other memorabilia of special times you've shared. Let it serve as a reminder of your history together.

CHAPTER SEVEN:
YOUR SPIRITUAL AWAKENING

"If you want a deeper, more intimate connection with God, you must learn to honestly share your feelings with him, trust him when he asks you to do something, learn to care about what he cares about, and desire his friendship more than anything else."

— Rick Warren

Search for deeper meaning in your life

Many women are on a quest for deeper spiritual meaning in their lives. They express the need for something outside of them to hold onto while struggling with the challenges of life — a guiding force to surrender to and trust. They find comfort in knowing there's something bigger than all of us; that there's some divine order to the universe. What many are discovering is that belief in a concerned, personal God provides a firm foundation for dealing with anything in life — a

sustaining force where they can go to find peace —
even when the world around them is in utter chaos.

Do you, like some, have a negative image of
God? Without a vision of a supreme, all-powerful,
yet merciful, loving God, you will continue to live
your life just getting by and living life day-to-day.
Midlife is your opportunity for a spiritual awakening.
To move beyond mere coping, you must develop
a connectedness with God. Everyone has an
instinctive need for God — a need to believe in
something larger than yourself that you can turn to
in times of crisis.

Adversity forces you to look to God and seek Him
for the peace and joy that will come by focusing
your thoughts on Him. When you worry, you allow
yourself to dwell on all the negative aspects of your
circumstances — the loss of a job, the death of a
loved one, the frustration over a teen's rebellion,
the criticism of a boss, or rejection by someone you
admire — instead of approaching the throne of God
with a grateful heart for sustaining you through
difficult times in the past. Your circumstances
don't need to rob you of your joy. When you're
grieving or deeply troubled, you'll discover that only
the peace that comes from God can soothe your
aching soul. Even in difficult situations, you can
experience joy!

By reading and meditating on Scripture, you
allow God to transform your thinking. He gives you
a new perspective on your situation so you can
greet your life with an eager expectancy. By putting
your faith and trust in God, you soon see the beautiful and exciting things He plans to do in you and
through you.

God's Word is active. It motivates you into action, encourages you to persevere, comforts you when you're hurting, and brings you hope for tomorrow. When you're brokenhearted, flipping through the channels on the television isn't going to bring you any lasting comfort. Sure, getting caught up in a sitcom or a romantic movie may temporarily dull the pain, but God wants to heal your wounded emotions and restore you to wholeness.

So many distractions exist in the world today — magazines, television, Internet, cell phones, advertising, movies, DVD's, video games, newspapers and tabloids — but what kind of life do they offer? What kind of hope or comfort do these things provide? The Good News found in the Scriptures offers everlasting life, not just after you die, but right now! It draws you closer to God and He, in turn, draws closer to you — equipping you with everything you need to live victoriously here and now. Anything that doesn't bring you closer to Him is worthless, without life.

What are you focusing on? What do you give your attention to? Are you allowing your mind to dwell on the negative circumstances in your life or are you meditating on the life-giving Word of God?

I feel strongest when I just hand over whatever is troubling me to God. I say, "God, I just can't handle this or even deal with it." And it all seems to be lifted off my shoulders and my heart is light. It's what keeps me happy and healthy mentally and physically. I couldn't imagine being without my faith...ever! It scares me even to think of going back again to the life I had without it. All that I went through before I had my faith in God was much harder to deal with and work out in my mind because I didn't have God's standards to follow. Now I have him to guide my footsteps and it's so comforting! —Jan

Surrender control of your life to God

Women in today's culture are striving to be completely self-sufficient, not wanting to put their faith in anyone beside themselves. While I encourage you to take responsibility for your life and not just let life happen to you, it is ultimately God who is in control. As more and more midlife women are admitting that they are powerless over their own lives, they are discovering true inner peace that only comes from a relationship with God. They feel centered and content to let God have control of their lives.

Know God's greatness and understand your need of Him. It's been said that you need to follow a brighter light than the glimmer of your own candle. How true! Recognizing God's ultimate control means surrendering your own control. God can accomplish amazing things with women whose hearts are yielded to Him.

When I figured out that my life wasn't really about me, I was set free. When I gave up control of my life to the One who created me, I was free to pursue my dreams, take risks, and fulfill my purpose. When I put my faith in God and His plan for my life, I was finally able to stop worrying about the future.

My life before forty turned out the way it did because I didn't take the time to ask God. —Luanne

It doesn't mean that life becomes easy; it just means that God knows what you need before you do. —Rosa

It seems to me I've been the strongest when I've admitted I couldn't handle something by myself. —Angie

> *There comes a time when you have to realize*
> *that there is a Higher Power and if you can*
> *move over enough, he can show you things*
> *that are possible.* —Ellen

Develop an intimate relationship with God

You belong to God, and He is desperately in love with you. Do you take time to know Him? As in any relationship, you need to spend intimate time together.

"The more I learn about him, the more I love him," observed my friend, Pamela, as we sat and had lunch together. "Everything Clark does just makes me more in awe of him." She gushed on and on about how well he cooks, his knowledge of English literature, his expertise on the tennis court and the volunteer work he does with Big Brother.

"I just can't stop thinking about him!" Pamela's exuberance over the man she'd been dating the past three weeks was truly enthusiastic, but it made me stop and wonder about my own relationship with God. Do I get that excited talking about God? Am I filled with wonder every time I learn some new aspect of His character? Am I truly in "awe" of all He's done? Do I demonstrate the same kind of exuberance for God as Pamela feels for Clark? When was the last time God and I even had a "date"? Would I possess the same kind of passion for God if I were as inseparable from Him as Pamela and Clark had been these last three weeks?

If you seek peace and intimacy with God each day, you will experience an even deeper relationship with Him than Pamela and Clark's newfound love for one another. If you ignore Him, however, you often can go days, sometimes even weeks, before you realize that the sweet communion you've experienced with God has been disrupted. Remember, you are as close to God as you choose to be.

Recognize evidence of God's presence when you see it and feel it. Spend time in prayer. Everyone has access to God. You can ask God for what you want. He loves you and wants to do good things in your life — and through your life to help others — but sometimes you have to wait on His timing. ✕

Sometimes God waits to answer your prayers because He wants to increase your faith. I can remember several instances where I had prayed for something to come about and believed in my heart that God wanted that situation for me as well. But I got impatient, took back control of my life, and tried to do it my own way — failing miserably! When I finally confessed my stubbornness and pride to God, He gave me what I had been praying for, but through His plan, not mine.

If you're familiar with the Old Testament story of Abraham, you'll remember that God promised to give him a child even though he and his wife were very old. They waited for many years and the promised child did not come, so Abraham and his wife decided that her servant would carry their child. This was not what God intended. Finally, when they repented and put their trust back in God, he blessed them with the son that they had prayed for so long.

Sometimes God doesn't answer your prayers the way you'd like him to because He can see the bigger picture and understands that it's not in your best interest. If you're a mother, you know the desire to give your children everything they ask for, but you are wiser and more experienced and can see that some requests would actually be harmful to them — or maybe you have an even better plan for them if they'd only trust you. It's the same way with your relationship with God. You need to believe that He loves you as a parent loves a child — but God's love is perfect!

God wants to share His abundance with His children who believe in Him and ask Him for his blessings. Have you stopped to ask God to expand your business? To restore your marriage? To heal a division between you and a close friend? To use you to make a difference in someone else's life? God can do all that and more. He changes hearts, transforms lives, and brings inner peace to your soul.

Morning devotions are really my key to keeping my life in balance; nothing goes right unless I talk to God first every day. —Joyce

I think women get more spiritual as they get older. I spend thirty minutes alone on the sun porch every morning quietly reading and reflecting; it grounds my day. If you get too busy, you don't have time to hear God speak to you. —Inge

My view of God has changed as I've gotten older. It's changed from a "holier than thou, do as I say" perception of God to a loving God who cares more for me than I do for myself. I also have come to believe that the negative things that happen to us open our eyes to the love of God. Everything bad that's happened in my life brought me to a point of saying, "Okay, God...I've had enough! Let's see what YOU can do!" There comes a time when you have to realize that there is a Higher Power and if you can move over enough, he can show you all the wonderful possibilities.

I came from a "God-is-gonna-get-you-for-that" upbringing to where I am today. I see God more as a loving, kind Father and Friend. I can talk to God much like I talk to my friends — at any point in the day. I don't have to be in a certain position: kneeling, dressed up, in church, or whatever. I know he hears me, and he always answers me even if sometimes the

> answer is "no." I used to think that I had to tell God how I wanted my prayers answered, but now I pray for knowledge of his will and power to carry it out.
>
> Life is much different when you walk with your Creator. You maintain a sense of inner peace and calm. I am often amazed at the spiritual truths I receive, how certain events work out, and answers to my most desperate needs present themselves when I least expect them. —Brenda

Seek spiritual guidance

God has your success story written out. Ask Him what it is! He will reveal it to you when you have ears to listen. As long as you continue down the path of self-dependence — despite any personal success — you will miss out on the reason for your existence.

Know that God has a plan for your life! Jeremiah 29:11 says, *"For I know the plans I have for you,"* declares the Lord, *"plans to prosper you and not to harm you, plans to give you hope and a future."* You were created for a purpose! Wouldn't it make sense to ask your Creator what that purpose is?

In March 2003, I sat down with my journal at an outdoor café in Anaheim, California, and wrote this prayer:

Dear God,
Please show me your purpose for my life. Give me your vision for how my life can be used to bless others. I want a dream that's bigger than me,

something that could only be tackled with you moving the mountains of impossibility out of the way. Thank you, Lord.

I didn't know back then what I would be doing, but I wrote in my journal, "I want to do something that will inspire others to improve their lives." As I write this chapter, I know that I have been allowed to see only a small glimpse of how God wants to use me (probably because if He revealed the entire plan to me right now, I'd be blown away!), but I'm excited about my vision and know that my humble prayer will be answered in an awesome way.

Before you can discover God's purpose for your life, you need to seek the One who created you. The following chapter goes into greater detail about determining your life purpose, but if you don't have a foundation of faith, you'll never discover your true purpose for being alive.

I'm a very pragmatic person. I'm not into organized religion, but I do believe there's a Power greater than us all. There's got to be a Supreme Being because there's absolute perfection out there. I believe the world is an absolute miracle! I've had experiences where I've been inspired, empowered and strengthened by that Power. —Libby

Discover the road to inner peace

Do you ever feel uncertain about what you are depending on spiritually for hope in your life? If you died tonight, where would you go? If what you believe weren't true, would you want to know? If so, I'd like to share some Bible verses with you that explain how you can have a personal relationship with God:

"For all have sinned; all fall short of God's glorious standard." Romans 3:23

Yep! That's everybody! You, me...your next-door neighbor — no one is perfect.

"For the wages of sin is death, but the free gift of God is eternal life through Christ Jesus our Lord." Romans 6:23

Wages are what you have earned or deserve. A gift is something that is unearned. Sin is the current condition of your life. God is the Creator of the universe. Death is the end of life here on planet earth and unless you connect with God while you are still alive, it will mean eternal separation from God. Eternal life is living with God — forever!

"Jesus replied, 'I assure you, unless you are born again, you can never see the Kingdom of God.'" John 3:3

That's right, no streets of gold unless you connect with God.

"Jesus told him, 'I am the way, the truth, and the life. No one can come to the Father except through me.'" John 14:6

Believing Jesus is God's Son and putting your faith in Him is the only way to a relationship with God.

"For if you confess with your mouth that Jesus is Lord and believe in your heart that God raised him from the dead, you will be saved. For it is by believing in your heart that you are made right with God, and it is by confessing with your mouth that you are saved." Romans 10:9-11

You actually have to open your mouth and tell God that you believe that Jesus Christ is the only way to erase all the bad stuff in your life so that you can have a relationship with Him!

"He died for everyone so that those who receive his new life will no longer live to please themselves. Instead, they will live to please Christ, who died and was raised for them." 2 Corinthians 5:15

Once you become a believer, you'll stop thinking about yourself all the time and be concerned about pleasing God.

"Look! Here I stand at the door and knock. If you hear me calling and open the door, I will come in, and we will share a meal as friends." Revelation 3:20

Jesus is knocking on the door of your heart. If you open your heart to him, He will live in your heart and start hanging out with you. Is that cool, or what?

If you get nothing else out of this entire book, it is my sincerest desire that you will open that door and let the One who loves you so much come in and have a relationship with you. It will change your life!

"*But those who hope in the Lord will renew their strength. They will soar on wings like eagles; they will run and not grow weary, they will walk and not be faint.*" Isaiah 40:31

Action Steps:

1. Answer these questions in your journal:

   - Are you a sinner?

   - Do you want to be forgiven?

   - Do you believe Jesus Christ died on the cross for you and rose again?

   - Are you willing to surrender your life to Jesus Christ?

   - Are you ready to invite Jesus Christ into your life and into your heart?

2. If you want to receive the free gift of eternal life, you must confess that Jesus Christ is the Son of God, repent of your sins, and accept his loving leadership and guidance in your life. You can do this by saying this simple prayer:

   > *Dear God, I have sinned against you. Please forgive me of all my sins and for living my life my own way, without you. I believe Jesus Christ is your Son who died on the cross for me and rose again. I want Jesus to come into my life and into my heart, filling the void that I feel inside. Please help me to live the life that you have designed for me to live. My life is yours to do with as you wish. This I ask in Jesus' name. Amen*

   Congratulations! If you have prayed this prayer, you are now a beloved child of God! Nothing compares to experiencing the power of God in your life. You will be amazed! I would love to hear from you so I can be praying for you as you begin this spiritual journey. Please email me at: christine@PathPartners.com

3. Find a Bible believing church and start attending worship services regularly. Your spiritual journey is enhanced by building relationships with fellow believers.

4. Seek out a beginners' Bible study. If there is an Alpha course being offered in your area, I highly recommend it! If you don't already own a modern translation of the Bible, I suggest you purchase a **New International Version (NIV)** or a **New Living Translation (NLT)**. Then start reading the Gospel of John. Just read a few verses every day and ask God to show you what He wants you to learn from those verses. It's called a "living" Bible because the Spirit of God that now lives in you reveals truths and insights to you that you might not otherwise see upon first glance.

5. Make a commitment to pray every day. Prayer is simply a conversation with God. Like any conversation, it's as important to listen as it is to speak. Don't be in a hurry. Take time to be still so you can "hear" God's voice. No, this isn't an audible voice (usually), but God's Spirit in you will speak to you and you will know it's Him. I cannot explain this, but it is a wonderful experience. Sometimes I will write my prayers in my journal to keep focused or when I have a particularly perplexing problem that I want His spiritual guidance on. I find that answers are revealed to me as I'm writing. Your journal will then also be a chronicle of your spiritual journey.

CHAPTER EIGHT:
"CAN YOU SEE ME NOW?"

"And the day came when the risk to remain in the bud was more painful that the risk it took to bloom."

—Anais Nin

Determine your life purpose

Midlife is ultimately about the search for personal significance. You sense there must be something more, and you start asking yourself, *"Who am I?" "Why am I here?" "Does my life really have a purpose?"* You hunger for meaning in your life — to feel in your heart that you matter and that your life is making a difference. You inherently believe deep down that life has more to offer, but if you merely go from one day to the next, doing only what is in front of you, it's like you are adrift on the rough waters of change without a guiding principle to steer you through the turbulent swells.

Reflecting on the lives of some of the most successful women who ever lived, you can see that they had a definite purpose and they knew it. Susan B. Anthony's purpose was *"to campaign for women's rights."* Mother Teresa, one of the most well-known and highly respected women of the 20th century, dedicated her life *"to care for and comfort the poor, sick and needy all over the world."* Harriet Tubman, creator of the Underground Railroad and who single-handedly helped more than 300 slaves escape bondage in the decade prior to the Civil War, existed *"to lead slaves to safety and freedom."* Clara Barton, founder of the American Red Cross, saw a need *"to obtain and pass out provisions to those in need."*

My purpose is *"to inspire women to lead productive lives with passion and purpose — at any age — through the spoken and written word."* You also have a purpose to fulfill — a reason for living, breathing and existing. Rick Warren, author of the best-selling book *The Purpose Driven Life*, says that your heart represents the source of all your motivations — your hopes and desires, your secret ambitions and dreams — the unique emotional heartbeat that races when you think about the subjects, activities or situations that excite you. You are enthusiastic when you are doing what you love to do; no one has to motivate you, challenge you, or check up on you. You do it for the sheer enjoyment.

The struggle for most of us is that we aren't clear about what our life's purpose is so we spend a lot of time attracting what we don't want into our lives. Once you discover your purpose, however, everything else will follow almost automatically. Your purpose becomes the systematizing objective around which you arrange all areas of your life. You can draw on it to fuel your vision, inspire your actions, and create a life of deep personal satisfaction and joy.

Michelangelo is most commonly associated with the Sistine Chapel, but his true love was sculpting. He would travel to the mountains in northern Italy to select the quality, shape, and size of the blocks of marble that he wanted to work with and supervise the quarrying as well as the transporting of them via ship back to Rome. There he would spend days just looking at a single block — walking around the marble, sitting and staring at it — until he would finally get his inspiration. Only then would he get out his hammer and chisel. When he was asked where he received his inspiration, he replied, "I saw the angel in the marble and carved until I set him free."

Just like the sculpture hiding in the block of marble, your life purpose is the underlying foundation that gives your goals direction and meaning. If you don't take time to define your purpose — your calling in life — any goals you may achieve lack cohesiveness. Like an all-encompassing umbrella, your purpose transcends your goals. Goals are crucial to achieving any kind of success, but goals alone are arbitrary and unsystematic. Goals are simply the steps you take along the way. In order to live life to the fullest, your goals need to reflect your purpose.

When you align your everyday goals with a well-defined purpose, you will enjoy peace of mind and a wonderful sense of being alive. Without this common thread holding your various activities together, you wander through life aimlessly. Discovering your purpose puts your life into crystal-clear perspective.

Purposeful work means that you care deeply about something. You don't feel obligated to perform; rather you are passionate about it. When you're serving a purpose larger than yourself, your level of commitment also expands. Purpose puts power and excitement in your life.

'I feel something is still missing in my life. I think it's because I haven't yet found what I am here to do. —Peggy

Discover your unique gifts and talents

The great scientist Marie Curie said, "Life is not easy for any of us. But what of that? We must have perseverance and, above all, confidence in ourselves. We must believe that we are gifted for something, and that this something, at whatever cost, must be attained."

You exist on this planet for a significant reason. Even though the earth is filled with about six billion people, you are absolutely 100 percent unique. No one else in the world is just like you. You have a distinctive combination of strengths and talents created and given to you that can potentially provide tremendous value to others. Anytime you use these God-given abilities, you are fulfilling your calling.

Sue, age 44, did what was expected of her for

years. Married at age eighteen, she pursued a teaching career. "One of my teacher's once told me, 'you're a sweet girl — you'd make a great teacher.' For years I lived a false identity based on what other people thought I should do."

Then she reached a turning point in her life when she started questioning all of her choices. She went back to school for interior design and discovered her natural gifts and abilities. "I love my work!" says Sue. "If I have a creative project ahead of me, I can't even sleep. It's not even work for me — I completely lose track of the hours."

Sue discovered that when you're redirecting the course of your life it can be difficult to get going, but once you're focused on how you want to live your life, the momentum created by your vision makes it much easier. "If you can just take a baby step, eventually it gets hard not to take the next step. The first step is so empowering."

So what unique gifts and talents do you have to share with others? The best way to discover these talents is through honest reflection on what you most enjoy doing. Ask yourself, "What am I doing when I lose track of time? What parts of my present job or life activities do I get pleasure from? What do I do well naturally? What do I daydream about? What would I do every day if my time were my own?"

Take a moment to look back on what you have accomplished in the past decade. In your eyes, what have been your ten greatest successes to date? What were you doing when you felt completely alive and "in the zone?" Your answers are indications of your purpose in life.

God shaped you for a purpose and He expects you to make the most of what you have been given. Don't rob this earth of your purpose by taking it to the grave with you. Only when you are truly contributing to the world in your own special way can you feel completely fulfilled. As the Reverend Oliver G. Wilson once said, "Use what talents you have; the woods would have little music if no birds sang their song except those who sang best."

I believe each of us is here for a reason and that the "something-is-missing" syndrome is actually a search for your purpose in life. I am grateful for my art; it gives my life the sense of purpose, personal satisfaction and deep fulfillment that I'd been seeking. It's my belief that we are only happy when we are doing what God wants us to do. —Martha

Dare to dream BIG

After thirty years working in an orthodontic office, Joyce, age 53, started a Mary Kay business.

"Mary Kay opened up a whole new world for me," Joyce claims. "I started really seeing the women around me and caring about how they felt about themselves. At first giving a total stranger my business card required me to step out of my comfort zone, but now I love meeting new people. Mary Kay is so much more than a cosmetics company. It's helped me grow as a person and my clients have become my friends."

One way to jumpstart that growth process is to reconnect with your childhood dreams. What dreams have you let die? Did you listen to the voices that said, "You can't make a living as an artist? Go to law school, settle down, and be responsible." Or maybe you started believing the voices that said, "You have to be really good to be a professional athlete...or musician...or dancer." Perhaps the financial resources weren't available for you to go to medical school, or you were needed in the family business, or you were told, "Women don't usually succeed in that field."

When we stop pursuing our dreams, a little piece of us dies and we become disheartened. What about the woman who trained to be an opera singer, or the woman who wanted to live and study in a foreign country? Stepping up and pursuing your dream rekindles that passion and zeal that everyone has the capacity for and lets us experience fulfillment.

Set aside some time to let yourself dream. You might want to be a wedding or event planner. Possibly you see yourself as a motivational speaker or a public relations consultant. Maybe you've always had the dream of writing children's books or romance novels. Whatever your dream is, live without regret!

How do you want your children to remember you— as a woman who sought all that life had to offer, using her gifts and talents to their fullest extent, or as a bitter, overweight couch potato with a victim mentality? Our children need to see that we dream, that we have the courage to strive for something better.

The reason people don't accomplish what they set out to do is because they lose interest. Their dream, their goal, is really not that important to them. Is the dream you are following important to you? Refuse to let your vision be suppressed by what appears to be "practical." Each time you stretch, you find yourself at the threshold of what simultaneously excites you and scares you. Tony Robbins says, *"People are not lazy. They simply have impotent goals — that is, goals that do not inspire them."*

For instance, I had the dream of writing a book for many years. It didn't happen, however, until I stopped just thinking about it and decided to actually do it. I told other people that I was writing a book, knowing that my pride wouldn't allow me to back out once I'd made my intentions public. It made me accountable if for no other reason than I wanted to avoid embarrassment.

Then I came up with a plan. I attended a publishing conference and read books on how to self-publish a book. I subscribed to online newsletters and talked with other self-published authors. I laid out the steps I needed to follow on a timeline. Finally, I planned how I would celebrate when I had my finished book in my hand. I imagined how it would feel, which in turn motivated me to keep going when I wanted to quit.

Are your goals big enough that they excite other people? Do they make you want to jump out of bed each day eager to get going? For example, if you have a goal of making enough money to "stay afloat" — how exciting is that? Is that going to make you jump out of bed in the morning, saying,

"I can't wait to get going, so I can make enough money to pay the bills!"? I doubt it.

The only limitations that exist are those we impose on ourselves. Elienne Lawson, a young woman who became completely deaf at the age of nine, went on to play the piano and learn seven languages! Our minds will believe whatever we convince them to believe.

What's stopping you from living your dreams? Most people are not living the lives they truly want to live because they are not thinking big enough and they're not clearly focused on exactly what they want to do.

Whatever you think about can become a reality — so be careful what you think about! Your beliefs create your life experience. You can change your life by changing your beliefs. In fact, it's impossible to create success without believing that you are capable of being successful.

For Leslie, age 45, a layoff was the impetus she needed to pursue her dream of starting her own training and consulting business, *Invest in People.*

"My definition of success is making a positive impact on someone else's life. The business has allowed me to do that. When I finally realized that I need to do things for me, I was able to say, 'This is who I am — how I dress, how I earn an income, how I live my life — like it or lump it!' I no longer felt like I had to live to please everyone else."

Focus on what you want more of in your life. Whatever you pay attention to tends to grow larger. The journey to self-improvement begins in your mind. Your thoughts, attitudes, and beliefs guide your behavior. Open the door of your mind to new possibilities; be willing to examine life from a new perspective. With an open mind and a desire to grow, transition can be a time to flourish and lead the abundant life you were created to live.

If you fail to consciously visualize what you want to create, your new situation will just perpetuate the mistakes of the past. You will remain in your "comfort zone" of experiences created by your standard of living, your peer group and their lifestyle, your willingness to risk and try new things, and your beliefs about yourself and about life. Stretch your comfort zone beyond its existing boundaries. The dream may not seem practical, but you must embrace it with commitment and a belief that it can be realized.

If you don't believe deep down that you deserve to have a specific goal or characteristic, or can't see yourself having it or being that person, you won't really go for it and do the things that it would take to get it. If you believe you can't do something, you probably won't be able to do it. And that's because your mind will be holding you back, discouraging you when you most need encouragement, setting up obstacles where there aren't any, or letting you give up when you need to persevere. If you believe your goal can be accomplished, your mind — and hence your behavior — will do nearly everything it can to help you succeed.

Mary, age 42, decided a few years ago to become proactive in her own life and took time to evaluate what she enjoyed doing — what made her heart sing!

"My only goal at the time was not to repeat my experience of being miserable. My mother died at age sixty-four, still waiting for 'her turn.' I knew I needed to become responsible for creating and nurturing a life that I designed for myself. You have to consciously live for each day because you don't know how many you'll have. You can't trust your happiness to other people because when they fail, you fail."

Working at a yacht club at the time, Mary was invited by one of the members, a textile artist, to help her set up a studio in Florida. "This woman taught me that I had value and I discovered that I had a gift for helping people get organized."

Things really do happen for a reason. In the airport, a man near her was having a heart attack. Mary performed CPR, but it was too late.

"The man died in my arms. It was a very moving experience," says Mary, "but the upside was that the airline gave me a free ticket for trying to save his life. The National Association of Professional Organizer's convention was only days away and now I had this ticket, so I went."

Today Mary owns her own business, *Within Reach Organizing Services,* and is living the life that she envisioned for herself.

"I've purchased a new home, a new car...and have created a backyard garden that relaxes and rejuvenates me. I give back to the community by doing a lot of volunteer work because I firmly believe that what you give out you get back, but on a different level. I'm actively growing my business and creating strategic alliances. One key factor in my success has been picking out people in my life that I trust implicitly and could be confident that they'd be on my team. My friend, Jan, will call just to check on me and let me know that she's there for me. Everyone needs to hear, 'You go, girl! Don't give up!' once in awhile."

If Mary had kept her eyes closed and hadn't been open to seeing the opportunities when they came, she wouldn't have the fulfillment that she is currently experiencing. She would not even have looked for any of these opportunities if she'd allowed her mind to think that she wasn't good enough or that it was impossible for her to attend the conference because she didn't have the money.

When you know what you want to do in life, when your vision is clear, the conditions enabling you to achieve it suddenly emerge. You find yourself encountering books, resources, financial support, mentors, partners, and other pieces needed to complete the "puzzle" comprising your vision. By holding your vision firmly in your mind, you will experience synchronicity at every turn. Though it will continue to amaze you, you will soon begin to anticipate it.

I've finally found my wings. Now I'm starting to play with them and see how they work. —Mary

Develop a clear vision

Carolyn, age 55, woke up on a cold Saturday morning in February fifteen years ago with an idea for a supplemental math curriculum.

"My daughters needed to stay brushed up on their math facts over the summer and I couldn't find what I wanted at Kmart or The Teacher's Store," explains Carolyn. "I called my sister and a longtime friend and we sat down and formed Tri-C Publications, Inc. It took us nearly three years to write the curriculum, develop a business plan, and figure out how to run a publishing company, but in 1991 we were finally open for business."

The three women relied heavily on their husbands' business experience.

"Rik's years in hospital administration proved to be invaluable," Carolyn says. "We also needed the guys to sign for our business loan. Initially it didn't bother us that the bank required their signatures, but as time went on and the banks still required it, we started to get annoyed. After six years of showing a profit, we thought we deserved to be treated as successful business women." Now of course, with sales throughout the United States, Europe, the Middle East, and Japan, they get the respect that's rightfully theirs.

"Due to my husband's work, we moved around a lot as the girls were growing up. It was difficult to make friends every time we settled in a new city," Carolyn says. "Cleaning my house or getting my nails done just didn't fulfill me. When I attended dinner parties with my husband, people would ask me if I worked outside the home. Even though raising my children is the most important thing I've ever done, people started treating me as though I had more worth as a person after I became a business owner. I honestly don't regret though one moment of staying home with my daughters."

"Owning a business has given me a lot more confidence in my abilities. I'm not a confrontation-

al person by nature, but I've learned to deal with
irate customers, fire employees, and switch ven-
dors when necessary," Carolyn explains. "We also
have more financial opportunities now. For
instance, we're in the planning stages of building a
cottage."

The income from Tri-C Publications also allowed
her husband, Rik, to take an early retirement from
the hospital and pursue his passion working as a
certified personal trainer.

What has Carolyn learned from the last fifteen
years? "Just roll with the punches," advises
Carolyn. "Embrace the positive and downplay the
negative. There's just so much to be grateful for."

To develop a clear vision, you need a strong
sense of purpose in life and the ability to dream big
dreams. Refuse to limit yourself to what's been
done before. Constantly test your own limits!

Only by having something to focus on — a mission statement, an affirmation, or a strong vision —
can women keep their heads above water when
everything around them is pulling them down.

In the vision phase, you generate the mental
images that ultimately become your next experience. When I moved to Chicago as a young, single
woman, I dreamed of living in an old brownstone
and hanging out with artsy type people. A year
later, I realized that I was living this vision — the
spacious apartment I lived in matched my imagi-
nary one, and my roommate was an actress who
frequently invited other actors over to rehearse
scenes.

Several years later when I left my career to stay
home full time and raise our children, I had a vision

for living in the country, raising much of our own food and being as self-sufficient as possible. It turns out I'm not the avid gardener that I'd dreamed of being, but we did manage to raise our own chickens, goats, and rabbits for several years. Our world is the result of these mental pictures, coupled with strong emotions, which bring each picture into being.

Effective vision statements share these characteristics:

- **Present tense** — "I am" vs. "I will be", "I have" vs. "I will have", "I feel" vs. "I will feel"

- **Open-ended** — leave room for something to happen that is even bigger than what you have imagined

- **Specific** — needs to be recognized when it happens, yet not so specific that you aren't open to other possibilities

- **Challenging** — must require you to stretch beyond your comfort zone without being unrealistic

- **Emotion-based** — must describe how you will feel when you have achieved your vision

Trust your own intuition — particularly if one idea, vision, or action step keeps recurring in your mind as the step you should take next. Discern your motives. Do you genuinely sense your vision calling you to take a step toward its manifestation?

Your vision represents how you want the next period of your life to look as the multitude of possibilities merge into a single, focused direction. Developing your vision creates a positive momentum as you move forward in that new direction.

Create a vision board

Last November, six forty-something women spent a weekend at a cottage in Northern Michigan to create vision boards for the coming year. We sat around the big kitchen table, fully equipped with stacks of discarded stock photo catalogs, travel magazines, and back issues of Oprah's magazine *O!* We spent Friday and well into the day Saturday cutting out pictures that represented the relationships, experiences, and achievements that we wanted to manifest in our lives.

As we talked, we shared our hopes and dreams for the future. When we had finished cutting out the pictures and words that represented the type of life that we wanted to live, we arranged them on poster board and then shared our finished collages with one another. It was an amazing, eye-opening experience! One member of our little group shared that she had manifested everything on a previous vision board within eighteen months of creating it. Talk about the power of suggestion! Our minds really do believe what we program into them.

Gather up pictures from magazines and elsewhere that depict the desires of your heart. Stock photo catalogs are great for this activity! Arrange them on a poster board and include positive affirmations. For instance, on my vision board is a couple I perceived to be going over their goals and dreams for the future. Under the photo, I cut a caption from a magazine that read, "The lessons about sharing clearly pay off." Another photo shows a woman working at her computer under which I placed the words, "Books that make a difference."

When you're all done arranging the pictures and

words on your board, glue them down and then frame your vision board! You want to hang it on the wall where you'll be reminded of it daily. Even if you don't consciously think about it everyday, your subconscious mind will continue to process the messages you've programmed for it to go to work on. (Mine is hanging over my workspace.) Each time you see the visual cues, ask yourself, "What small step can I take today to achieve my goal of...?"

This is why, in order to succeed, you have to monitor your thoughts closely. Wherever you focus your attention — wherever you put your energy — that is what will grow.

Set a goal to accomplish something in the next ninety days that you never thought you would find the time to do. Is there one thing that you have always wanted to do, but you have not yet had the courage to try? If you make a clear goal and begin to take the next apparent steps toward its realization — whatever steps are required to convince your subconscious that you are serious about focusing on that goal — you will soon find you have reached it.

People say they want to be happy, but they seldom plan to be happy. Instead, many women fall into the trap of, "When my kids leave home," or "When my husband gets his promotion," or "When we're out of debt," *then* I can be happy. It doesn't work that way. If happiness is your goal, then you need to decide to start being happy today. Not tomorrow, not in a week, not when "X" happens. Today!

I'm very driven. I keep written goals — on the refrigerator, the nightstand, and even my computer at work. If I don't have a visual, I lose sight of what I'm trying to do. My current two-year goal is to raise $5-10K to participate in a 3-5 day bike ride in three different parts of the country. The money raised is donated to AIDS research. When a cause is something that's important enough to me, I find a way to make it work. NO EXCUSES!!! —Maureen

Action Steps:

1. Write a movie script, in the present tense, of your perfect day and provide as many details as you can.

2. Write a letter to yourself from some point in the future. For instance, if you're forty now, write a letter from your eighty year old self and see what wisdom you learn.

3. Sit alone quietly and reflect on what it is you truly desire to be, do, and have in your life. Get clear about what you truly want (what you feel real enthusiasm for) and make a plan, a mental picture complete in every detail.

4. Write what you don't want. This will help you get clear about what you do want. Afterwards, write the positive of every negative thing you can come up with. For example, "I don't want to be over-weight" becomes "I want to be in great physical shape."

5. Write at least one action you can take right now to move toward your goal. What simple step can you take immediately?

CHAPTER NINE:
"YOU GO, GIRL!"

"The victory of success is half won when one gains the habit of setting goals and achieving them. Even the most tedious chore will become endurable as you parade through each day convinced that every task, no matter how menial or boring, brings you closer to fulfilling your dreams."
—Og Mandino

Move confidently into action

Ruth, age 57, embarked on a journey eighteen months ago that few of us have even dreamed of doing. She and her daughter, Laurel — a single mom with two children — moved to Cancun, Mexico, and started a boat touring business. Ruth is the only woman boat owner in Cancun and probably all of Mexico! Their voyage has been a treacherous one with many setbacks and heartaches along the way, but the strength Ruth has discovered inside herself has been priceless.

Widowed unexpectedly at forty-nine, Ruth was filled with grief and despair. After several years of mourning, her daughter insisted they take a vacation to Cancun. "I fell in love with the place!" exclaims Ruth. "It was like coming home!" Three months later, she returned to Cancun by herself and stayed for ten days. "I told myself, 'I have to find a way to live here.'

"I had worked for an orthodontist for twenty-one years, but then a management company purchased his private practice so I quit and cleaned houses to survive. After my second visit to Cancun, I talked to Laurel about moving here with me and opening up a bed & breakfast. We came down here a year later to look for property, but became very discouraged by what we found. By Thursday, we decided to take a break from our search and went out on a boat. We met Palemon, the captain, and stayed and talked to him after the excursion, picking his brain about the boating business. By the time we returned to the States, we had a new direction, renewed hope — and many hurdles to get over."

First of all, Laurel had to get the court's permission to take her children out of the country. Despite overwhelming odds against them, the judge gave his blessing on their plans and it deepened their resolve. Ruth took out a home equity loan and found an attorney to set up their corporation. There were still so many things left to do. The two women had to find a Mexican partner, locate a boat to purchase, hire a boat surveyor, find someone to transport it to Cancun, look for a place to put their boat, and obtain proper permits from the harbor master.

Meanwhile Laurel, a newly certified diver, met
someone online, Kevin, a man they affectionately
refer to as "our angel." Although Kevin and his wife
now live in New Jersey, they had previously lived in
Cancun for twelve years and not only spoke the
language, but they also understood the customs.
"Kevin helped us tremendously with laying out a
business plan, designing our website, and even lent
his assistance in dealing with the harbormaster,"
says Ruth, with awe still in her voice. "Furthermore,
he never took a dime for all his work."

Despite warnings from family and friends, as
well as being strongly cautioned by the experts they
consulted, Ruth and her daughter decided to make
the leap of faith. They loaded up Ruth's travel trailer
that she'd previously used for hauling horses and
left for Cancun after Laurel's children got out of
school in June.

"Getting through the border was in itself an
adventure," laughs Ruth. "We looked like the
Beverly Hillbillies loaded down with all our worldly
possessions. We actually had to pay a border bro-
ker to help us get through the ordeal." The border
patrol still cut open several of their packing boxes
and sorted through the contents of their trailer
until they were finally satisfied. By dinnertime, they
were at long last allowed to proceed after spending
most of their day going through customs. "We still
had a five day drive from the border to Cancun
ahead of us and my Rottweiler wasn't the least bit
happy with the trip. Finding a place to park the
trailer didn't make it any easier either. We finally
arrived in Cancun on June 26, 2002. It was a beautiful drive — mountains, lush green grass — you'd

be driving along and little towns would pop up out of nowhere.

"It was an amazing thing to see — just a simple way of life. The people had so little, but were so happy. People in the States have so much, yet they are miserable. It's so sad." Her grandchildren (ages 11 and 15) have adapted well and within two months, both were speaking Spanish fluently.

Business got off to a slow start, however, and they actually came within a week of packing up to go back to the States when a local tour company picked them up and now represents their boat tours to tourists staying at resorts in Cancun. They take tourists out to a reef for snorkeling and then to a local island for lunch and an afternoon of shopping and sightseeing. Business hasn't been booming since it's so dependent on the weather, but it's definitely picked up. Their old friend, Palemon, is now their captain and they found Pablo, their jovial first mate and bartender.

"I've been back to the States a couple times to visit family and friends, but Cancun is now my home. Someday I think I'd like to open a dude ranch here. I thought for a while I'd be able to bring my horse down here, but she wouldn't have adjusted well to the tropical climate."

Ruth and Laurel have had several more hurdles to jump over since they arrived in Cancun, but Ruth says, "Even though it's been very, very difficult, this experience has made us a lot stronger and our faith more personal. Going to church and reading the Bible means so much more to me now. I find myself talking to God several times a day and seeking his guidance. If we're down here only to strengthen our faith, then this endeavor has been a success.

"In life, we spend so much time making other people happy, sometimes you have to stop and decide what's going to make you happy. You can sit back and say, 'What if?' but if you don't try, you'll never know. We only have one life to live."

In order to achieve her dream, Ruth had a clear vision of what she wanted to do with her life. Once your vision is clear, you are ready to move confidently into action. With the momentum generated by your vision, it is time to determine your first step, however small, and begin moving toward it with optimism and a sense of adventure.

One step leads to the next, often in unexpected directions, and you are on your way.

Begin with what you have right now and make today count by taking a new step toward your most important goals and dreams for the future. Consider what initial small step you can take that will move you closer to your goal. How can you break down your goal into daily tasks?

Discover the "better than zero" rule. Any action is better than none. If you skip a day because you don't have enough time, you'll lose momentum. So if your goal is to write a book, write a page every day. If you want to get in shape, walk a mile every day. If you want to study a new subject, read a chapter every day.

Celebrate your actions (going for a walk every day for a week) as well as your results (losing two pounds). This is important because you can control your actions much more than you can control your results. What matters is that you're taking action every day. Taking consistent action will create a wave of positive momentum that will build your confidence as it propels you toward your goal.

Have a clearly established plan that you can begin working on immediately. Develop it step-by-step, but don't insist on knowing the entire plan in advance. Your plan will very likely only cover the first and possibly the second phase of the journey to your goal. As you begin executing your plan, other steps required to complete your journey will be revealed at the right time. It's easy to get over-whelmed. You only need a clear idea of the direction in which you are heading and the first move you can make toward your goal. Move forward and take action in spite of the fact that you don't have all the answers yet.

Act on the momentum your vision has created while your emotions are high and the idea is still strong, clear, and powerful. Don't let the feeling pass! You may intend to get your pilot's license, but if you don't call and find out about lessons when the idea first crosses your mind, the initial excite-ment starts to diminish. A month or two goes by...and then a year...and then you make excuses about all the reasons you couldn't possibly get your pilot's license anyway.

It's so easy to put off starting something new. After all, the daily demands of your current life con-tinue while you make the preparations to launch your new life. That's why during the crucial stages of a life transition, you need to run on two tracks at once. So buy the paints, enroll in the class, go to the seminar, schedule the appointment, or join the club before the idea passes and the emotion gets cold. By quickly taking action, you've increased your motivation.

> *I got to the point where what I was doing wasn't what I wanted anymore. That is a pretty big realization. The really hard part though is deciding to do something about it. — Candy*

Know your motivation

Women are highly motivated when something means a great deal to them. If a woman falls into deep water and doesn't know how to swim, she will become highly motivated in an instant! Why? Because now there is something this woman wants more than anything else in the world. She wants to survive, and nothing had better get in her way! A woman gasping for air will become one of the most excited and enthusiastic people imaginable! So it is with us all. If you want something bad enough, you will find enough energy, excitement and drive to relentlessly pursue it.

Many women have found themselves suddenly alone with a need to support themselves and sometimes children too. Most women in these circumstances are highly motivated to tap into their creativity and discover unutilized talent and abilities that will allow them to not only survive a financial and emotional crisis, but also thrive under these new circumstances.

What drives you? Discovering your basic motivation allows you to generate the energy needed to follow through with the nitty-gritty, disciplined work that is often an essential part of achieving a goal. By the way, thinking you "should" do something only serves to create guilt when you don't follow through. That's because "should's" come from somewhere outside of you. In the long run, you can only be successful if your motivation comes from inside.

View your transition from a longer time perspective — what will be the impact of this action in twenty years? Is that the outcome you want?

Generally speaking, lack of motivation is at the root of your procrastination. There are two ways to motivate yourself: You can fear the consequences of not taking action, or, you can get excited about the rewards and benefits of being proactive. Vividly imagine all the rewards and benefits that happened because you took action and didn't hold back! Sense the feeling of accomplishment and feel good about challenging yourself to a higher level of performance.

List all the positive reasons why you want to or must reach this goal. Then list all the things you will miss out on, be forced into or dislike about your life if you do not achieve your goal. A motivated person is far more willing to step outside their comfort zone and take that all-important, life-changing chance. They become more, they do more, and thus they have more.

Do "whatever it takes"

The entrepreneur Mary Kay said, "One of the secrets of success is to refuse to let temporary setbacks defeat us."

Be persistent. Adopt a "never give up" attitude.

Persistence is one of the most important qualities of any successful person. Persistence means "steadily pursuing a course begun in spite of opposition or discouragement." It means never giving up. It means picking yourself up after you fail, dusting yourself off, and trying again.

Be willing to do "whatever it takes" — any obstacles in your way don't matter. Some women mentally take themselves out of the game by getting caught in the trap of perfectionism. They procrastinate and make excuses instead of doing what needs to be done to move their dreams forward. If you wait for perfect conditions, you'll never accomplish anything. Accept that you're likely to make mistakes. Learn as you go. Don't lose your momentum.

Decide what it is that you want out of life and then stick to it relentlessly. Devote yourself to that passion and don't get sidetracked. The average person bounces from task to task throughout the day, without being very conscious of which tasks are more important than others.

Sometimes things don't go the way you originally planned, and some days you just don't feel excited or motivated to take another step forward. These are the times when you force yourself to focus on what you want to achieve. You choose to reconnect with the reasons why achieving your goals are so important to you. You choose to have faith in yourself and take action, no matter what is going on in the world around you.

Force yourself to make the distinction between "I can't" and "I won't." When you achieve these little successes, they will spur you on to even greater challenges — so you benefit both from completing the task and from getting more motivation for the bigger ones. So stop waiting until you lose ten pounds, your kids leave home, you retire, you get married, you move, or you have more time. Take action now!

I started a business, stood up to my grown children, and finally set some boundaries that should have been set years ago. I started doing things for me, things that I enjoy doing. I continue to recognize and express my individuality instead of letting those around me dictate how I should look, act, and think. For instance, I dress and wear my hair the way I want it and not how someone else likes it. My outward appearance is only a reflection of the changes that have taken place on the inside. I have learned so much about myself! —Abby

Overcome fear and self-sabotage

Do you have reasons or excuses for not meeting your goals? It's not uncommon for us to confront setbacks, to have things not turn out as planned, to find ourselves sabotaging our own efforts, or to feel paralyzed with fear at the prospect of letting go of a familiar lifestyle. It's important to avoid taking a setback personally. Recognize the event as something temporary. Instead of saying to yourself, "I'm a failure," say, "This is just something that happened."

If you hit a slump, remind yourself of a major accomplishment. When you doubt your own confidence or ability to move ahead, recall past risks or challenges and how you overcame them.

What have you done in the last five to ten years that you're really proud of? Did you run your first 5K and finish? Did you take a class and discover a new interest? Did you meet a deadline that was a real challenge for you? Maybe what you need to do is take the advice of explorer John Goddard, *"When I get stuck, I restart myself by focusing on one goal I can finish in the next seven days — something simple. I don't think about anything else. That usually starts my momentum again."*

It's not uncommon to unwittingly stop ourselves by focusing on our fear or by sabotaging our own progress. Our next area of growth is the thing that scares us yet also excites us more than anything else!

Fear causes us to feel helpless, depressed, weak and sick. It is not the event that is causing all the trouble, but it is the fear of that event. Fear of failure can be avoided by not trying, but then we will gain nothing.

You need to develop the ability to act as if the things you want to accomplish in your life have already occurred. This reinforces both your conscious and your subconscious mind so that you begin to react to situations and attract those people who support your goal. Conversely, if you don't believe or trust that you can and will make it happen, you will remain stuck with your old lifestyle. For some women, staying in their comfort zone while clinging to their fear of change is exactly what keeps them from growing.

Our beliefs determine our experience. Thoughts like "I'll never be happy" or "I can never win" will manifest themselves in our lives. We can tell our subconscious something we want it to believe, and it will absorb that new thought. No judgment — just acceptance. We have to do it over and over again, however, because our subconscious likes familiar stuff. After a while, our behavior changes.

If you're constantly thinking, "I'm so stressed," you will reinforce that belief. You have a choice; you can alter your perception of your world if you put new words into your subconscious, such as "I can handle it" or, even better, "I thrive on this!" Remember, misery is optional.

The first step is discovering what you normally say to yourself. Program your words using only the present tense. If your subconscious receives "I will be happy," it assumes that this feeling will happen some time in the future. You can change your perception of a situation and your creative mind will help you think of ways to have your dream become a reality.

When your plate is full of stress and responsibilities, sometimes it's just easier to avoid examining some of the unpleasant realities of your life — whether it's dissatisfaction with your career, your weight, your marriage or something else entirely — and simply carry on with business as usual. Indeed, many people make their way through life surrounded by a bubble of denial and self-deception. —Sarah

I finally realized that I needed to start pleasing myself and discover what makes me happy. I've found that it's all right to say "no" sometimes. —Kim

Stay flexible

Periodically, it's a good idea to stop and evaluate whether or not the path you've chosen is the right one for you — or even if you're still on the right course. It's so easy to get distracted by other opportunities that come along.

It's okay to decide that the course you started out on needs to be modified. In fact, in many cases, it's a good idea to monitor your progress and determine if adjustments are necessary. Don't be afraid to adjust your vision when appropriate whether due to new information, a change in motivation, or a change in circumstances. You need not feel guilty for failing to follow through on a vision that may now be outdated. Your vision might have changed. You need to regularly ask yourself, "Is this still what I want?"

Did you know that Apollo flights from earth to the moon were off their chartered course ninety percent of the time? The same is true in life; we get distracted and pulled off course. The amazing result, however, is that they reached their destination — by constantly correcting their course. They stayed close enough to the path to reach the target as planned. Rather than being on a perfect course, they were on a critical course. Within it there is room for mistakes and corrections.

Women who find the critical path toward their vision expect to make course corrections along the way. "On course" does not mean perfect. On course means that even when things don't go perfectly, you are headed in the right direction.

To avoid drifting away from your focus, ask yourself at regular intervals, "Is what I'm doing right now helping me to achieve my goals?" –OR– "Did this action take me closer to my vision or further away from it?" Pay attention to the results that follow from your choice. If they did not further your vision, modify your action and be willing to make a new choice.

Action Steps:

1. What is your number one goal that you want to achieve in the next three months? Create a step-by-step plan for accomplishing this one goal.

2. Break down your step-by-step plan into daily tasks. Write two weeks worth of action steps into your calendar. Start with today.

3. Make a list of ten reasons why you must reach this goal and what it will do for you to have reached it.

4. Create a list of daily rewards and a big celebration for reaching your ninety-day goal.

5. Assuming you have accomplished your goal already, what impact will this make on your life in five, ten, or even twenty years? Is this what you want?

CHAPTER TEN:
GIVING BACK—THE TRUE
PATH TO ABUNDANCE

*"We cannot hold a torch to light another's
path without brightening our own."*

—— *Ben Sweetland*

You were put on earth to make a contribution

Tess, age 49, came from a large, rural family with ten children. She married her high school sweetheart at the age of seventeen after discovering she was pregnant. She and her husband, Roger, have now been married for thirty-two years and are the parents of four adult daughters.

"When the girls were little, I started a dried flower business," says Tess. "I loved it, but after several years the market started to get flooded so I looked for something else to do. I knew that if I didn't start working on something while those kids were growing up, I would be lost. Those girls were my whole life — I absolutely loved parenting!"

Deciding to pursue a master's degree in psychology, Tess attended graduate school full time for two and a half years, choosing to take an extra semester in order to earn a specialty in drug and alcohol counseling. She finished graduate school just as her girls were graduating from high school. After two years, she started a private therapy practice. "I love what I do!" exclaims Tess. "I'm exhausted at the end of the day because I put so much of myself into it, but I really don't mind working the extra hours."

Tess has been fortunate that her work enables her to help others through private practice, seminars and now through her book, *Flying by the Seat of My Soul.* With the success of her book, requests for Tess to bring her light-hearted, whimsical, yet deeply moving stories to audiences has taken off. She particularly enjoys the opportunity to speak to cancer survivors and others dealing with life-threatening illnesses.

"If I can show people how to have fun — even when the world around them looks bleak — then I feel like I've fulfilled my calling," she said.

Instead of discovering how to get the most out of life, you were created to enhance life on earth. Instead of asking, *"Who's going to meet my needs?"* ask, *"Whose needs can I meet?"* This gives your life greater significance and value. Anytime you use your God-given abilities to help others, you are fulfilling your calling. In fact, you are only fully alive when you're helping others. Only when you are truly contributing to the world in your own special way can you feel completely fulfilled.

In *The Purpose Driven Life,* Rick Warren writes, "Don't settle for just achieving the 'good life,' because it doesn't satisfy. You can have a lot to live on and still have nothing to live for." Real abundance is about more than having a lot of money and material items. Many extremely wealthy individuals do not enjoy real abundance. They are never content with what they have and live in fear of losing it.

And yet you don't need to reject material wealth or shun the blessings that come with it. Many good things can be accomplished with money, eliminating much unnecessary suffering in the world. Money can give you a measure of freedom from the control of others. It can give you time — time to appreciate the simple things in life more fully, time to develop your gifts and talents, and time to build and nurture your relationships. Money can also give you the power to make a difference in the lives of others. If you look to money for fulfillment, however, you are sure to be disappointed.

I realize that I've spent a good portion of this book trying to get you to pay attention to your own needs. That's because until you love and respect yourself, you can't truly give to anyone else. With maturity, however, you will again be aware of the needs of others, but without the self-sacrificing, martyr syndrome that characterized your "giving" in the past. This time you'll be able to give out of your own abundance because your cup will be full.

Everyone has something to give

Libby volunteers as an intake coordinator at the Women's Resource Center. Typically the women she sees are recently divorced or widowed and come to the center for help during their transition.

"I'm the first contact these women have," she says. "I'm a huge advocate for women becoming the person they were meant to be. They'll be happier and so will those around them. If their husbands aren't supportive of their dreams, they should move ahead anyway. I don't believe anyone has a right to deny someone else's personal growth. My husband knew from the beginning that he'd met an unconventional woman — he knew that I'd do things anyway! I'm respectful of our relationship, but I am also respectful of myself."

One of life's best-kept secrets to achieving abundance in every area of your life is giving. Giving is extremely powerful because it affects us mentally, physically, emotionally, and spiritually. Without a doubt, giving can have a profound impact on your life. Only by giving are you able to receive more than you already have.

Everyone has something to give. For some women, it's out of their pain. An article in my local paper featured a young wife and mother who had been raped at knifepoint ten years ago. She and her husband decided to go through with the resulting pregnancy and now have a beautiful daughter that they love very much. This remarkable woman has now written a book about her experiences to help other women deal with a similar trauma.

Scores of organizations have been started over the years as a result of a woman's personal crisis or trauma — M.A.D.D., the Samantha Project, and many others. Maybe you don't know your purpose yet, but right now you can start by sharing your knowledge and skills. Everyone knows something that can improve someone else's life. What you know may not seem significant to you because you may do it without effort. Perhaps you could teach literacy, offer your nursing skills, or assist low-income families on how to design a budget. Seek to make a difference with the gifts and abilities you've been given.

Chances for Children is one example of a non-profit organization that partners with agencies who have a proven track record in the areas of child-related healthcare, education, protection, and advocacy. It's their objective to rescue "forgotten children" — those who are homeless, affected by the HIV virus, or in other ways disadvantaged. Their goal is to help these children become self-sufficient, productive members of society.

You probably remember one or two special teachers or professors who aided your journey through school. They are most likely the individuals who gave above and beyond what was required by their job description. How can you impact the lives of the people you come in contact with in your daily life? You have more to offer than you think.

My main purpose for many years was to help raise useful, productive Christian daughters, but you have to reinvent yourself as a woman once your kids move out of the house. Since the children no longer consume all of your energy, women struggle to know what to do next. There's so much to choose from! —Sharon

Commit random acts of kindness

Small gestures can have a far-reaching impact. Live your life in such a way that others are touched. Each person you touch passes on the kindness and caring to another person, and in this way, your actions have a ripple effect even though you may never know what the end result of your actions will be.

A movie released in the year 2000 starring Helen Hunt, called *Pay It Forward,* was based on this concept. It's about a young boy (Haley Joel Osment) who attempts to make the world a better place after his teacher (Kevin Spacey) gives him that chance. The movie's premise was "when someone does you a big favor, don't pay it back...pay it forward!" The rules were:

1. It has to be something that really helps people.
2. It must be something they can't do by themselves.
3. When you do it for them, they do it for three other people.

You cannot be self-absorbed, living only for yourself, and expect to live an abundant life. By reaching out and making someone else's life a little easier, a little happier, a little more joyful, you open the door for more abundance to enter your own life and you are able to feel happiness in ways that you could never imagine. As Helen Keller once said, "True happiness...is not attained through self-gratification but through fidelity to a worthy purpose."

Invest time and energy in a cause that serves a larger purpose

Become a contributor, not a spectator in life. Women who replenish their spirit by investing emotional energy and time in a cause that serves a larger purpose gain a deep sense of fulfillment. What you give becomes an investment that will return to you multiplied at some point in the future. No matter what your financial status is, you can make a difference by giving your time, energy and ideas to the charities and programs that mean the most to you.

How about helping to move children out of poverty? Now you can participate in addressing the housing crisis that is faced by more than twelve million children. The Women Build training program seeks to further the mission of Habitat for Humanity International by teaching women how to build decent, affordable housing with Habitat affiliates everywhere. Since 1991, women crews have built more than 350 Habitat houses in the United States.

Women-built projects provide an opportunity for women to learn construction in a supportive, non-intimidating environment. On a Women Build site, women feel more comfortable and are willing to tackle all aspects of construction and, given the right training, quickly become skilled.

If you'd like more information, visit the Women Build Web site at **www.womenbuild.com** or to locate a local affiliate, contact Habitat for Humanity International's Women Build department at **womenbuild@hfhi.org**.

> *I am a changed person and have said good-*
> *bye to the old me and am embracing the new*
> *me.* —Joy

Leave a legacy

Is it possible for one idea to change the world? Absolutely! If you're willing to dream big, you can make the world a better place.

It was more than fifty years ago that Danny Thomas, at the time a struggling young entertainer with seven dollars in his pocket, got down on his knees in a Detroit church before a statue of St. Jude Thaddeus, the patron saint of hopeless causes. Danny asked the saint to "show me my way in life."

Gradually, the idea of a children's hospital took shape. His dream was to create a unique research hospital devoted to curing catastrophic diseases in children. More than just a treatment facility, it would be a research center for the children of the world.

Danny's dream — St. Jude Children's Research Hospital — opened its doors in 1962 and is now recognized as one of the world's premier centers for study and treatment of catastrophic diseases in children. To date, St. Jude has treated more than 20,000 children from across the United States and 60 foreign countries.

The remarkable part of all this is that all patients are treated regardless of the family's ability to pay. St. Jude's now has daily operating costs of approximately $923,026. A friend of mine, Frank Lunn, is pursuing his vision of raising one million dollars — about one day's operating costs — out of gratitude for the hospital's treatment of his young son, a leukemia survivor. Danny is gone, but his legacy goes on in the hearts of people like Frank who attributes St. Jude's with saving the life of his child.

Albert Pike said, "What we have done for ourselves alone dies with us; what we have done for others and the world remains and is immortal." What will be your legacy? Whose life will you touch today?

I have come to a very important milestone. For once in my life, I feel that I know myself and I can make clear, concise decisions about what I want and don't want. Because of the changes that have occurred at midlife, I am enjoying life more now than before. I am much more aware of who I am and where I am going. My constant striving to change has diminished and I am finally comfortable with who I am. My life is much slower than before and I am totally enjoying it! —Ellen

I grew up with very low self-esteem. My first husband literally put me through charm school so I could hold my head up and 'fake it.' I never dreamed that I'd someday be speaking to an audience of five thousand people at a convention. —Luanne

My mom taught me to be a very compassionate person. I have volunteered at the Humane Society and helped out with various programs like Project Angel Tree and Kids' Club at church. I think it's good to expose Eric to giving back, although I do try to limit myself to one community activity at a time. —Maureen

Action Steps:

1. Research different charities and/or local organizations where you can get involved. List five organizations that you might consider assisting. Do they have web sites? Check them out with the Better Business Bureau. Then choose two or three to call. Have them send you their information, including how much of their funding actually goes to helping people. When you find the one you think is best, ask how you can help. Even if you can't contribute financially, there are often other ways you can lend a hand.

2. Teach in a literacy program, serve in a soup kitchen, or sort donations at a homeless shelter. If you're an animal lover, you might try the National Humane Society. If you appreciate public television, you might want to help with their next fundraiser. If you have a heart for battered women, you might offer your services at a domestic abuse shelter. Volunteer your time until you discover a project or a cause that truly blesses you.

3. Look for ways you can commit random acts of kindness. Fill someone's parking meter, let someone go ahead of you in line, or simply open the door for someone. You'll soon discover that you've become addicted to how good these small, seemingly insignificant acts make you feel. If nothing else, it gets you thinking about someone else beside yourself.

4. Go on a mission trip to a third world country and help build houses, attend to the sick, or spend time with a needy child. It will dramatically alter the way you see the world. Or help the Red Cross or other disaster relief organization after a flood, a hurricane, or a tornado. Work side-by-side with the victims as they pull debris from their homes and try to salvage what little might be left. Provide comfort to those who are suddenly homeless. You will be blessed beyond belief!

5. Ask other people how they're giving back to the world. You'll be amazed at how many women you know who are actively involved in projects and causes — and one of them may be just right for you!

CONCLUSION

"Whatever you want to do, do it now. There are only so many tomorrows."
—Michael Landon

Your journey into midlife can be awkward, confusing, and difficult. My hope is that reading and working through this book has helped you battle the powerful urge to "run away from it all" and given you a new perspective on what's really important in your life so that you can make choices that reflect your true priorities.

Learn to trust the process and have faith that the best is yet to come. Be gentle with yourself, however, and expect setbacks, distractions, and emotional roller coaster rides as you deal with the inevitable losses that come with this time in your life. Use this as an opportunity to create a life based on your own interests, passions, and dreams. Make a spiritual connection that will give your life new meaning and strengthen you for the rough times still ahead.

I have confidence in your ability to rise above the loneliness of the "empty nest," the grief of losing a loved one, and the heartbreak of a broken relationship. In turn, I know you will discover wonderful, supportive relationships with men and women alike as you learn to let go of limiting beliefs and be honest about who you are and what you need to be fulfilled. I anticipate that you will emerge from your "crisis" with new hobbies, careers, and businesses that reflect your personal desires and talents. As you release any subconscious need to be a victim, I trust you'll be willing to act in your own best interests — allowing yourself to live a life that you know in your heart is right for you.

I challenge you to dare to dream big dreams and look forward to all the possibilities life offers you. Find ways to get involved in the community and give to causes that are meaningful to you. Continually aspire to make a difference with the gifts and abilities that you've been given. My greatest hope is that you'll determine now to embrace midlife and discover that abundant living is rich, satisfying, and full of achievement. Simply, it's living a life that counts — *so bring it on!*

I see myself aging and notice the fine lines are appearing. I am increasingly aware of no longer having what I took for granted all these years. As I notice these things, I am forced to look inside at my true beauty that comes from an acceptance of the things I cannot change. It comes from being at peace with my life and facing the future with great expectations. I believe your inner beauty comes from having confidence in the path you're on and knowing your future will unfold as it was meant to.
—*Wendy*

Christine would love to hear from you!

If you have an encouraging story to share of how you have used the principles outlined in this book or comments on how Bring It On! has inspired you, please write to the author at:

Path Partners
PO Box 434
Rockford, MI 49341

Or send an email to:
Christine@PathPartners.com

Give Bring It On! to your friends and colleagues!
Check your local bookstore or Order Here

☐ Yes, I want ___ copies of Bring It On! for $14.95 each.

☐ Yes, I want ___ copies of the Bring It On! workbook (available Fall 2004) for $12.95 each.

☐ Yes, I want ___ combination packs of Bring It On! with the workbook for $24.95 each.

☐ Yes, I would like information about starting a Path Partners group in my area. Please send me information.

☐ Yes, I am interested in having Christine speak or present a Path Partners workshop to my group, association, or organization. Please contact me.

Include $3.95 for shipping and handling. Michigan residents add 6% sales tax. Allow 1-3 weeks for delivery. **Please inquire about quantity discounts for orders of five or more.**

Name _____

Organization _____

Address _____

City/State/Zip _____

Phone _____ E-mail _____

My check or money order for $_____ is enclosed.

Please charge my ☐ Visa ☐ MasterCard ☐ American Express ☐ Discover

Card # _____

Exp. Date _____

Signature _____

Make your check payable and return to:

Path Partners
PO Box 434
Rockford, MI 49341

Or order online at:
www.PathPartners.com

Phone: (616) 246-8594
Fax: (616) 588-6374

If you'd like your book(s) personally autographed by the author, please clearly print the name(s) you wish to have in the inscription. Thank you!

Christine - 40